ISBN 0-8028-0702-X

The epigraphs that appear on pp. 11, 26, 31, 54, 168, and 185 are taken from the *Psalter Hymnal,* 1987, and used by permission of CRC Publications, Grand Rapids, MI 49560.

Unless otherwise indicated, all Scripture quotations are from the HOLY BIBLE: NEW INTERNATIONAL VERSION. Copyright © 1973, 1978, 1984 by the International Bible Society. Used by permission of Zondervan Bible Publishers.

A Path through the Sea

One Woman's Journey from
Depression to Wholeness

Lillian V. Grissen

WILLIAM B. EERDMANS PUBLISHING COMPANY
GRAND RAPIDS, MICHIGAN

With deep gratitude
to
God

for the three men who brought me
from breakdown to breakthrough:

my psychiatrist,
Dr. Gelmer Van Noord, now in heaven

my pastor,
Rev. Henry DeMots, now retired

and, most importantly,
my husband Ray

Contents

Foreword

DEPRESSION IS SOMETIMES referred to as the common cold of mental health. Everybody gets it at one time or another. For most people, depression, like the common cold, runs a normal, short course and ends without need for special medical or therapeutic care. For some people, depressive spells seem more complex and more frequent, and talking things out with someone is helpful. For a smaller number of people, medication, with or without talking things out, is essential.

Depression perhaps more than any other condition shows the marvelous and constant interplay in human beings between body, mind, spirit, will, genetic inheritance, social and religious environment, and individual life story.

In courageously writing her story, Lillian Grissen has shown us how all these factors woven together produced a profound depression in her. She describes movingly the five-year period of pain and darkness that changed the course of not only her life but also the lives of her husband and children. She lets us see the process by which she was led to face the roots of her pain, of her perfectionism and excessive guilt. She describes the family and religious environment of her childhood in detail but without bitterness or blame. She is careful to point out that the same message or teaching given to different children will be received differently by each child, since each child hears and responds differently. She describes, again without bitterness, how the expectations of her as a girl were automatically and rigidly different from the expectations of her brothers.

If severe depression is complex, the healing of it is also complex. Lillian gives full credit to her pastor, to her psychiatrist, who was a Christian, and to her husband, Ray, who gave her constant loving support even during times when she could give nothing back.

Lillian's story will encourage many people who suffer. Those of us who know her now see her as a leader, a writer, an educator, a gentle feminist who loves God and who loves her church. The story of her emergence from the prison of perfectionism, rigidity, and despair is a testimony to the patience and gentleness of the Spirit of God, who works within us, often using human means.

"Why should it take so long?" we may ask. "Why doesn't God heal when we ask him?"

The answer, I think, lies in the respect that God has for the means of healing he has allowed us to discover in creation, and also in the respect that God has for us as individuals. God knew Lillian in the most profound and most biblical sense of that word. God loved her for who she is, and God is never an abusive lover. God does not impose healing on people. In the words of Ecclesiastes, there is "a time to kill, and a time to heal; a time to tear down, and a time to build up." God respects and blesses that rhythm. And in the fullness of time, healing comes.

Lillian's husband, Ray, adds an account of his experience of her illness that will help spouses of those who struggle. He includes some very practical advice for family members and friends who would like to help but don't know how.

Lillian is careful to point out that her story is not intended as a prescription for others, not even as a generalized description of depression. Treatment for depression has changed since the time of which Lillian is writing, though the factors in cause and recovery remain similar. But it is one woman's authentic and courageous account of a profound struggle with her life and her God. It will inspire many.

Mary Vander Vennen
Psychotherapist and Director of
Professional Services
Christian Counselling Services
Toronto, Ontario

Preface

I TELL MY STORY for two reasons.

First, just as Christ cared for people who suffered both physically and emotionally, so psychiatrists, especially Christian psychiatrists and mental health workers, heal the human agony of mind and heart. Although the healing that comes from psychotherapy is not, of course, equivalent to salvation through Jesus Christ, committed Christian psychiatrists treat human pain as Christ did.

Spiritual taxidermy has emptied the word *depression* of much of its pain and has stuffed it with hackneyed myths and bromides. Often the acute suffering of depression, particularly that of clinical or deep depression, is viewed as punishment for personal sin. Yes, our creatureliness, which is distorted because of sin, is involved, but the healing of medicine and therapy can restore the suffering heart and mind to wellness.

The second reason I tell my story is that I believe it may be a "secret" that many Christian daughters of Christian mothers unknowingly share with me. This secret can be between father and daughter, mother and son, or father and son as well, but mothers and daughters are particularly vulnerable to the relationship, or lack of it, described here.

In *The Blessing,* Gary Smalley and John Trent make this observation: "In an explanation of the priestly benediction, 'The Lord bless thee and keep thee' (Nu. 6:24), one rabbi wrote, 'May the Lord bless thee with sons, and keep thee from daughters because they need careful guarding!'" This describes how my mother felt about me. As culturally appointed sentry, she sometimes wearied of guarding her only and recalcitrant daughter. She believed, as many Christians traditionally have, that the role of women is strictly limited by God, and she raised me accordingly. She did not know that her fervor implanted in me not only a legalistic brand of Christianity but also bacteria that would attack my heart, soul, and mind, so that eventually I would descend into a very deep depression and need extended hospitalization.

Each child born into a family has a story to tell. I am sure that each of my brothers has a different story, but this one is mine; I lived it. At the same time, it is a story that will be familiar to anyone who has had experiences like mine. In *Telling Secrets,* Frederick Buechner explains, "The human family all has the same secrets, which are both very telling and very important to tell. They are telling in the sense that they tell what is perhaps the central paradox of our condition — that what we hunger for perhaps more than anything else is to be known in our full humanness, and yet that is often just what we also fear more than anything else."

My secret is not important because I tell it or because it is mine. Perhaps, though, readers who are suffering from depression or are living with a person who is ill with depression will recognize themselves in parts of this story.

I pray that my story may encourage you to believe that there is help and hope, for the God of this universe, whose footsteps are not seen, has his path in the sea. And on this path is the exodus from the bondage of depression to a rich life, abundantly free.

Prologue

The boundary lines have fallen for me in pleasant places;
surely I have a delightful inheritance.

Psalm 16:6

A RATHER LARGE GROUP had come to the train depot in Grand Rapids, Michigan, to say good-bye to Ray, me, and our three children: Ken, four, Donna, almost three, and Susan, sixteen months. Good-byes are never easy, and many of us cried. It was April 1952, and we were headed for New York, on our way to the mission field in Africa.

In New York we boarded a steamer to Rotterdam, then traveled by air to Kano, Nigeria, and finished our journey to Lupwe by truck and barge. Lupwe is a small compound in Nigeria, British West Africa (Nigeria gained its independence in 1957 and became known as Nigeria, West Africa), where a contingent of our denomination's missionaries had served for many years.

At last, after a year of praying and planning, we had arrived.

We had come eagerly. Our denominational World Missions Board had appointed Ray to supervise any construction needed on the field and to maintain its buildings and equipment. He would teach and train Nigerians so that eventually they would no longer need the white man's help. The board had also directed him to relieve, where possible, the frontline missionaries from work that often took them from the prime task of spreading the gospel of Jesus Christ.

Neither of us had gone beyond high school, but my husband had several years of training and experience in many skilled trades. We were delighted to be accepted as missionaries and convinced that this was God's plan for us.

Ray loved his work, and his crew, ranging from twenty-five to thirty men, loved him. He did well, and the training program he began developed nicely. I was involved too, even though wives were not assigned specific tasks on the mission field.

I enjoyed living in Lupwe. I often felt, with the psalmist, that "the boundary lines have fallen for me in pleasant places" (Ps. 16:6). The pace of life was slower here, and it offered opportunities I had often imagined. Getting to know and learning to work with the people, especially the women, excited me.

One challenge was learning the Hausa language, which is known as the "trade language" of Nigeria. At first I had to study the language simply by hearing it and repeating it. This frustrated me. It seemed so inefficient, so unreliable to learn a language this way. There was no written grammar, the other missionaries told me. "Learn it the way a child learns. Imitate the sounds and patterns." All of them had learned Hausa that way. Our son Ken, not yet five, picked up the language easily and often became our interpreter. But this was not the way I learned best. I needed to know the whys and wherefores so that I could compare patterns visually and logically and not just orally. Fortunately, a few months later, we found a written grammar for Hausa. That made learning the language simple, and soon I could teach a women's Sunday School class. I loved the women and enjoyed teaching them, and I became friends with many of them. Besides talking about the Bible stories, we compared our children, customs, and food and discussed the things that Christian friends are interested in.

Homemaking took most of my time. Usually this satisfied me. Looking after three young children, and later four, and managing the house demanded my full attention, even though we had three male servants. Mazawaji cooked our meals and washed the dishes; Haruna did the housework; Yamusa carried the water and washed and ironed our clothes, and sometimes baby-sat the children. It took me as much time to supervise my servants as it would have taken to do the work myself. But since I had none of the modern conveniences I had enjoyed in the States, the housework didn't appeal to me.

The kitchen was Mazawaji's domain; I never entered it. A mud brick hut, separated from the back of our house by a few feet, contained a wood-burning stove that had no thermometer. Even though we had brought hundreds of cans of food and dried milk with us, we ate a lot of locally grown food, which Mazawaji prepared. He baked a good loaf of bread, even though he first had to sift the flour through double thicknesses of nylon curtain material to remove the weevils. When we had eggs, he also made good pancakes.

We bought our meat from itinerant Fulani herdsmen. Meat was cheap then — one British pence for one ounce of meat, any kind. But it came from cattle that were too weak to continue the long trek to market. The Fulani killed these weak cattle and sold the meat to the white people who lived close to the path to market. When beef wasn't available, we ate goat. Using a meat chopper, Mazawaji ground most of the meat, which was lean, dry, and tough. He mixed it with canned bacon, imported from England. Preparing three meals a day and searching the area once a week for one or two fresh eggs that people were willing to sell took all his time.

Since there were no restaurants within hundreds of miles, we missionaries were expected to host all visitors, both British and American, who came to Lupwe for various reasons. I had not expected to entertain at the high British standards practiced by the veteran missionaries in our compound. When my family and I arrived at Lupwe, we were hosted for several days — there were gracious hostesses, lovely tables, fine tablecloths, good china and glasses, several courses of food, and, of course, servants. All very British. Back in the States, I had wondered why missionaries on furlough had suggested that I bring our 100-piece dinner set. Now I knew. Most of our china, though, had been broken in transit, and I had to rely on my dependable plasticware. In addition, we had the only children on the compound; they failed to observe the niceties of British customs and manners.

Haruna was our houseboy, a young man whom I judged was much more comfortable in a hut than in a house. We didn't communicate too well, but he smiled anyway. He often swept the dirt and sand from one corner of the room to another, sending a fine cloud of red dust over window openings and furniture. Several times I showed him the right way to use a broom and a dustpan. He grinned and finally shook his head in understanding. From then on when Haruna "finished" sweeping, he scooped onto the dustpan what little dirt he had accumulated and flung it with a flourish into the dirt path beside the house.

Ready water demanded an ever-ready water carrier. A very necessary daily shower for a family of five and later six required that Yamusa frequently fill the metal barrel that Ray had perched above a shower stall he had built with wood from our packing crates. We poured a little water into a basin to soap ourselves completely before we allowed any water to drop from the barrel. Yamusa spent most of each day walking — not too rapidly, because it was hot — to the well, about three-quarters of a mile away, returning each trip with two filled buckets. That, plus washing our clothes by hand and pressing them with irons heated on a woodstove, took most of Yamusa's time. The children loved him, and when he wasn't hauling water or washing or ironing clothes, he played with them and guarded them possessively. I never worried about the children.

There was much that I enjoyed about this lifestyle and the work we were doing. But mission regulations were authoritarian, picky, and stifling. The small size of the Lupwe contingent — eleven adults and our three children — accentuated personality differences. At times relationships were ragged. Although these experiences cured me of my romantic ideas about missionaries, they did not diminish my conviction that indeed my lot had fallen in a pleasant place. God had given me a beautiful family and special work. What more could I want?

Still, when I became pregnant with our fourth child, I became uneasy. Little did I dream that this was a foreshadowing of events that would change my interpretation of God's Word, my philosophy of life, and my life itself.

A Path
through the Sea

A Rude Awakening

Where can I hide, where can I flee?
There is no place you do not see.

"Lord, You Have Searched My
Life and Know," stanza 2*

I STILL RECALL that awful morning in early February 1954. I awoke in terror, buffeted about with whiteness. Not the soft, billowy purity of marshmallow clouds, but a ghastly toadbelly white. As though enclosed in a steel accordion, my head pushed and pulled with excruciating rhythm.

I opened my eyes. The apparitions surrounding me gradually became nurses. The walls of the room pressed in on me, stifling me. Thoughts throbbed in my brain as I tried to be rational. Husband. Children. Where are they? Where am I?

Slowly it dawned on me. I was dead, but still breathing. I was in a hospital. A mental hospital, where they put crazy

* Copyright © Calvin Seerveld, Institute for Christian Studies, Toronto

people. The uneasiness of the early months of my fourth pregnancy had developed into full-blown angst as my child's birthdate drew nearer. What I had dreaded the months before and after our last baby was born had taken shape.

They had won. I had lost.

They had succeeded. I had failed.

They had me where they wanted me — jailed inside a mental hospital.

Bitterness overwhelmed me. Tears, unabated, did not wash it away. Like a cancer, the gall penetrated every nerve, muscle, and cell of my brain and body. When Ray visited me later in the day, I attacked him:

Why am I here?

Where are the children?

Why did you do this to me? I told you this would happen, and you promised me that it wouldn't. You promised I wouldn't be sent here. Why are you breaking your promise? What have I done that I have to be imprisoned here?

If the children are so well taken care of, you don't need me. I'm no good to anybody. Why can't I die?

Why should I live?

Ray's eyes were anguished.

We had come back to Grand Rapids about a week earlier. Two nights ago, Ray told me, my headache had been so severe that he had called the family doctor. The doctor came and gave me a shot of morphine, and I fell asleep. But when I awoke in the morning, the excruciating pain had returned. Our doctor advised Ray to see a doctor at Pine Rest, a Christian psychiatric hospital in Grand Rapids. *(Only crazy people went there; I had learned that in my childhood.)* Together with my father, Ray visited the psychiatrist, Dr. Gelmer Van Noord, who convinced Ray that I needed hospitalization. *(A lie. All I needed was some pills to squelch the pain in my head.)*

I didn't remember being admitted. I was there against my will. My pain, anger, and bitterness knitted themselves into an ever tighter net of despair around my body, my brain — and my soul. I could not stop crying.

When Ray left, quietly sad, I was desolate. I had told him to go, but I wanted him to stay.

What a failure I am. I wish I were dead. I couldn't eat. I was too tired.

The doctor, accompanied by a nurse, came to see me early that evening. He tried to assure me that everything possible would be done to help me, that nurses would always be there to assist me. The two of them left after that, but the nurse returned shortly and injected something into my thigh — to help me sleep, she said. But I didn't sleep. *I knew that drug wasn't for sleep. They lied.* Before morning a millennium had passed.

The intense pain in my head had subsided into a severe headache. *Maybe they'll let me go home.* After bringing a tray of breakfast, which I refused, the nurse returned to help me bathe. *A bath? Why must I take a bath? Why must someone help me?* The attackers within me had regrouped and struck ferociously. As I got up, my legs wobbled and my knees caved in. The nurse steadied me gently. I resented that, but I had to accept it. After helping me with my bath, the nurse sat me in a chair while she readied my bed. Then she put me to bed and tucked me in. *I may be crazy, but I'm not a child.*

Thoughts avalanched painfully through my head. Here I was — a young Christian woman with a fine Christian husband, four healthy children, and a calling that many would envy. And I had botched it! I had failed my husband and my children. My parents. My family. My church. But worst of all, I had failed my God . . . if he still was my God. Here I was, imprisoned in a mental hospital, when only a few weeks earlier I had been on our church's mission field in Nigeria.

There was no clock in my prison. *They don't want us inmates to know that time passes.* I had my wristwatch, but its minute hand never moved, not even when I shook my arm to see if my watch was still running. I was suspended in time, hanging in nothingness. I was dead, but still breathing. Dante said it much better: "I did not die, yet nothing of life remained." Life avoided me, and death did not want me.

I looked around. The door of my room had a peephole large enough for an all-seeing eye, I supposed, that couldn't see my pain, only my boorish behavior. Panic attacked me. They had no business putting me in a hospital without my permission. Without my knowledge. It wasn't fair. I wanted out. I sobbed and wobbled down the hall, tried the door, and found it locked.

I couldn't control my feelings, but I was also unable to act on them. I was furious, and the pain in my head was merciless. I felt guilty because I was so horribly angry. Good Christians don't lose their temper, I had been taught. I hadn't done that often during my adult years — not because I was a good Christian but because the physical price for my outbursts was too costly. The resulting pain in my head usually immobilized me for one or two days.

I stood at the door, crying. I was bone tired, joint tired, mouth tired. A nurse gently turned me around, took me to my room, and helped me lie down. She left, but returned moments later to give me an injection. I fell asleep.

When I awoke, a couple of hours later, I was sweating. What was happening to me?

Case No. 5352

Can you see, Lord, I am crying?
Do not spurn my sore unrest.
I pass by like those before me,
yet I claim to be your guest!
No more sadness — give me gladness,
be my hope before I cease.
Lord, dear Lord, I beg for peace.

"Once I Said, 'I Must
Keep Quiet,'" stanza 5*

THE ONLY BRIGHT SPOTS in my life were my husband's visits. Ray visited me every day, sometimes twice a day. I learned that a few days before my admission, he and my father had spoken at length with the doctor about me, Case No. 5352. Many years later I saw my "case history." This is how the doctor began his notes:

*Copyright © Calvin Seerveld, Institute for Christian Studies, Toronto

5

— Development: Normal intellectual and social life
— Mental characteristics: Bright, good-natured, serious, strong likes and dislikes, sociable, ambitious, persevering, very meticulous
— Adult life: Occupations, steady. Habits, regular. Domestic life, wide range of interests. No diseases, no injuries.
— Ages of children: Six years, four years, three years, and the fourth one, six months.

All of the family have been taking anti-malaria drugs in Africa and the patient has also.

Patient is very precise and meticulous in her work and in her appearance, "just like her mother." She is so to the extent that "it creates some problems in the home at times."

. . . [Patient] began to complain [in Nigeria] of difficulty in remembering things, and she actually did forget things that ordinarily she would remember. . . . It was thought for awhile that it might be due to anti-malaria drugs, but he [husband] thinks now that she was forgetting things because she didn't pay attention to things as she did before. Her work began to suffer and she became very slow at it. She complained of being tired and that it took her a day to do less than an hour's work. She began to lose interest in things ordinarily interesting to her.

Just before Christmas her husband had to go away for a week's trip to [another part of] the mission field. He took all of the children along, including the six-month-old child. The patient went to live with some friends in order to give her a rest. When he came back she did not seem to be any better. In fact, he thinks she was worse.

She began to worry about losing her mind. She looks

at coming into the hospital as a patient as the end of a missionary career that had hardly gotten started.

Husband says she felt better when she had something to do, especially if it had to be done, even though she had become very slow in doing it. This slowness would annoy her greatly. When she stopped working she began to complain that she [was beginning] to think about herself, and she didn't like to think about herself.

She then began to complain of being too tired to move. She began to worry about not getting the missionary work done, particularly the secretarial-bookkeeping work, which had been her responsibility while the regular bookkeeper was on furlough.

Patient cries easily when she talks about herself and sometimes when she talks to anyone. Everything began to seem too much for her, including talking to other missionaries. She began to accuse herself bitterly and vigorously about taking on too much work — which was done against the advice of others on the mission field. She, therefore, feels that this illness is of her own making and is her own fault. She accuses herself of not being satisfied with four children and a husband to care for [and needing] to do more than that in order to make herself more important. She therefore now feels that the mission of her husband and herself is a flop, a failure, her fault, and she fears meeting people. When people come she becomes silent, but she seems fairly well at ease when alone with her father or mother or husband or maybe two of them. When more than two or three of the relatives come, she becomes entirely silent. She also fears that she did strange things while she was on the field.

She would like to think that all of her difficulty is due to anemia, but she tells her husband there must be more to it than that as she knows they would not send her away from the mission field for anemia, which probably could be corrected on the field. She would seek psychiatric help and wants help if that seems necessary, but she fears that entering a mental hospital would be a one-way ticket out of mission work. . . . She believes she might be able to go back to mission work if she only would not be sent to a mental hospital.

Case No. 5352 was simple. Ray was optimistic. Fatigue, tension, too much work — all had taken their toll on me, he said. He suggested to the doctor that he and I could take a trip without the children, since they were being well cared for by friends and relatives. Maybe we could go to Florida, where the sun would be shining.

The doctor didn't say no. He merely said, "You can go on a trip if you wish. But, remember, you'll be taking Lil along — and her problems. She's sick."

The only trips we took were to the hospital.

Little did either Ray or I realize the extent to which my "problems" would take over our lives for the next five years.

Hope's Thief

The Lord gave and the Lord has taken away.

Job 1:21

DEPRESSION IS AN ILLNESS with many faces; it is complicated. To the sufferer, clinical depression is emotional, physical, and/or spiritual bankruptcy, with no Chapter 11 that allows beginning again. Much has changed during my journey over the last four decades, but clinical depression has not: it is still bankruptcy, intensely personal and excruciatingly painful. It is a lonely, private hell. People have easy answers:

Snap out of it.

Trust in the Lord.

Get right with the Lord.

Take a vacation.

Forget about it; stop thinking about yourself.

It's just an excuse.

She's just lazy, that's all.

It's all in your head; it can't hurt you.

But easy answers are false. Countless writers have tried to answer questions about depression. Countless self-help books are testimony to the desire of millions to cure themselves. No single theory covers all the diagnostic possibilities. Some writers are experts, and others are not. I'm not an expert; I'm simply an example.

There are no easy answers, but there is hope, much hope. Depression is curable. Early on my psychiatrist said to me, "Lil, the field of psychiatry is new. If now were ten years later, I would probably use different methods." Maybe. But the symptoms today are the same as they were during the 1950s, when I suffered from major clinical depression. Many schools of behavioral theory and psychiatric treatment have arisen since then. Most are based on humanistic views, and non-Christian psychiatrists, like non-Christian physicians, have been able to help thousands of people overcome illness. But Christian psychiatrists, psychologists, and social workers are best equipped to help depressed Christians.

I was indeed blessed. My doctor was a committed Christian psychiatrist. He was guided by principles that rest squarely on the truth of God's love and by sound mental health principles. His help not only put me on the path to recovery but also changed my life.

The help I received has enabled me to live a rich, happy, and fulfilling life, and has led me to mental, emotional, and spiritual health far beyond that which I had enjoyed before the onset of my illness. This book is my testimony.

At first, however, I didn't perceive my psychiatrist as a godsend. I saw him as an enemy.

My Own Fault

My sinful folly brought me low;
bowed down, I groan in anguished grief.
I have no strength, for I am crushed
and spend my days with no relief.

Helen Otte, "Rebuke Me Not in
Anger, Lord," stanza 2
(Psalm 38)

I AGREED WITH THE DOCTOR that wherever I might go, my problems would go with me, because I knew they were of my own making. The more I thought about my problems and myself, the more I hated me.

I didn't want to talk with the doctor. I didn't trust psychiatrists, I told him when I began to speak to him, and I certainly didn't trust him. People, especially Christians, who live right don't need psychiatrists. "Talking with me bothers you a lot, doesn't it?" he asked quietly. "Why?" We sat there and said nothing for what seemed like hours.

I hadn't asked myself why. I had brought my "condition" upon myself, I told the doctor. God's way wasn't sufficient for me. And if that was so, then I must be an unforgiven sinner separated from him.

During my pregnancy and after the birth of our daughter Anita (up until a couple of months before we left Nigeria), I had been very busy with my family and my work. I had always believed that a woman should be able to do more than *just* care for her family. Besides, I had servants. Not that I wanted a paid job or a career. But Christians are called to serve, aren't they?

I was doing the mission's bookkeeping and secretarial work when I began to attack each task with frenzy. My life was like a cassette tape on fast forward. At first I didn't *feel* ill. I relished each accomplishment. When my husband told the doctor what I had accomplished while we were in Nigeria, he replied, "That's a sure sign that she's ill. She was trying to hide from herself. But the time comes when a person's resources are overdrawn. Then she's just like a car that runs out of gas: it simply won't go."

The doctor was right. My work camouflaged my illness. I didn't *have* to do the mission's bookkeeping (during the regular bookkeeper's absence). I didn't *have* to answer every letter within a couple of days. (During the two years we were in Nigeria, I had written about a thousand letters — it was a way to keep missions in people's minds, I told myself.) I didn't *have* to take the language examination (my husband was the *real* missionary). It was just my ugly ambition to excel.

"I've always tried to excel," I told the doctor. "All my life I've set goals, made schedules, and prepared agendas for myself, and usually I couldn't accomplish them in the time I allotted. But this time I've gone too far. I've made a mess of everything." I had used up every ounce of my energy. I felt like I was losing my mind. I had become very forgetful, and my brain felt like dry Jello mix dissolving in hot water. When I started to cry, the doctor handed me a box of tissues.

"Are you able to pray?" he asked.

"No. That's the trouble. I can't. Besides, God doesn't answer me anyway. If he did, I'd still be in Nigeria. No use asking him to get me out of this mess. It isn't reversible; it's already happened. I'm like a fly caught in a spider's web, and the worst part is that I crawled into this web myself."

I hadn't wanted to return to the States. But I had had no voice, no choice. I was the victim of a conspiracy between my husband and Lupwe's medical missionary, Dr. Joyce Branderhorst DeHaan (many years later I thanked her for her part in the conspiracy). "I know I was slow, but I'd have gotten that bookkeeping done. But they didn't believe me, and they wanted me out of there," I complained to the doctor. But in my next breath I contradicted myself. "Maybe I wouldn't have gotten the work done. I'll never take another job again. I botched this one badly enough."

"I'm so sick of myself," I added. "I can't take care of my children. I can't talk with people. I can't stand to be with anyone except Ray. I can't read. I can't work. I can't pray. I can't sleep. I can't eat. I can't get interested in anything. My head hurts so much that I can't think. I don't know. I just don't know." And the tears flowed again.

"God is punishing me because there's so much *self* in me. He's punishing me for my pride. And he's punishing me for another mistake I made while I was in Nigeria. Sometimes I left all four children, even the baby, with a servant so that I could write letters or work on the bookkeeping. The other missionaries in our compound were shocked. They made their disapproval very clear to me. It's obvious I don't even know how to care for little children."

"You think you're here because you did so much work,"

the doctor said, "and you certainly did accomplish a lot. But maybe, just maybe you worked so hard because you didn't want to face the inner problems that are surfacing now. Our behavior always has causes and reasons, even when we don't recognize them."

I had never thought of that, but I didn't believe him. I knew how sinful I had been.

The doctor made these notes about our conversation:

> She says that there were periodic difficulties between various persons on the mission field. [I told him about several problems among the missionaries.] She says there always are because the missionaries live so closely together. Before this, however, she took things such as these difficulties in stride and they were straightened out, but things seemed to be altogether different when she took on so much work that it was a burden to her, and she rationalizes this by stating she took on this work so that she wouldn't think about the problems on the field [that affected her husband primarily].
>
> Impression: This woman is clear and well oriented without delusions or hallucinations. She has good contact with reality, realizes what has been going on and what her behavior has been. She has some insight, is intensely self-accusative, has become excessively fatigued and with [that fatigue] has come depression and spiritual inhibition and despondency.

"This is enough for today," he said. "I'll see you again soon."

Oh, no you won't. I returned to my room. My conscience flogged me for tarnishing the image of the mission field. Before Ray and I had gone to Nigeria, I had romanticized "foreign missionaries," and I didn't want to destroy that positive image

14

for others. How could I have said what I said? I would not talk again.

I wanted to die.

Hitting Bottom

My God! O my God! Have you left me alone?
Why have you forsaken me, deaf to my groan?
I cry to you daily and plead late at night,
but you do not answer or pity my plight.

"My God, O My God," stanza 1*

THE INTERMINABLE days and weeks became an endless month. I felt consumed by guilt and shame. Maybe there are reasons why people behave the way they do, as the doctor had said, but that didn't excuse my present conduct. What I needed was forgiveness — forgiveness for messing up Ray's life, our children's lives, and our position on the mission field. But who could forgive any woman for feeling so sad when her blessings were too many to count? Not God, surely.

I hated the endless nights, and I dreaded the mornings. Each day was a pit into which I slithered until I could go down

*Copyright © Calvin Seerveld, Institute for Christian Studies, Toronto

no further. Once I reached bottom, I couldn't climb back up. It seemed my arms and legs had no bones to support me. I was trapped in an abyss of sadness. God was showing me that once you fall that far, you're lost forever.

I wanted death — or not so much death as the oblivion of death. What was death, really? I wasn't experiencing *life* — or if it was life, then I wanted no part of it. I thought about many possible ways to die.

My brain was twisted. My emotional life, shattered. My spiritual life, demolished. My physical life, anguished. My suffering was masochistic. I was worthless — and shouldn't worthless things be discarded? Hadn't the Gospel writer Luke said, "The ax is already at the root of the trees, and every tree that does not produce good fruit will be cut down and thrown into the fire" (3:9)? I was already dead. Suicide made sense.

I knew that it was too late for God to forgive me. And I wasn't even sure any more if I wanted to be forgiven. I just wanted out. I was the injured party; the other missionaries I had worked with had hurt me. Yet I was the unforgiven one. My hospitalization was proof that God (if he did exist) was punishing me.

Ray and I continued to receive letters from our colleagues in Nigeria, kindly intentioned but mostly agonizing for me. On my birthday I received a dozen long-stemmed red roses from the person who had hurt me most. My body shook. I tore each rose into shreds and threw the pieces on the floor.

Quitting life. Being done with it. *Ray and the children will be better off without me.* Beyond that I thought of nothing, no one — except Cain. He too tried to excuse himself from his misdeeds. But he didn't get away with it, because God could see his heart. When he tried to blame his sin on God or Abel, he found it didn't work. Whatever made me think I could erase my slate by blaming others? I alone was guilty. I alone was

17

accountable for my behavior and ingratitude. God doesn't accept excuses.

Death was my way out. But Christians don't look at death that way. I had been taught that life and death belong only to God, but I argued that God didn't exist. If he didn't, why should I continue my miserable existence? What difference did I make to anyone, here or in eternity — if there is an eternity? If this God did exist, surely he wouldn't notice that one of the people he had rejected had slipped away from this huge planet with its millions of people! It was grandiose of me to even think about being *worth* anything to such a God.

I had no other way out. All roads of life were blocked. All escape hatches were closed. My hell had no exit. But again — there would be no mercy. I could not entirely put aside the idea that God might really exist, and then what? I still had a whisper of belief that said, yes, there is a God — a God of vengeance, the God of my childhood — and he would judge me, even though he had rejected me. The words of a song I had learned in elementary school flitted through my mind: *"You cannot hide from God."* I still would have to appear before the judgment seat I had learned about in childhood. I shivered.

I felt as though I were crouched naked before God, a dazzling entity who killed any sinner that stood before him. Although I felt dead in both body and soul, I simultaneously felt the pain of a creature being scorned by her Creator. Hell couldn't be worse. I was alone, and the loneliness, like shrinking steel armor, crushed me.

I remember the day that my longing for death was at its strongest. I was standing in front of the window of my room. In the distance I could see cars speeding by, filled with people who were free to go where they wished and do what they wished. Close by I could see some buildings, but mostly just the lower trunks of pine trees — a regiment of stern soldiers, ready for action. The trees were so tall that I would have had to raise my eyes to see the green of the branches, and my eyelids were too tired to do that.

It was dark and gray, an ordinary winter day in Michigan. The snow-covered ground, showing its black, satiny soil in patches, beckoned me. I was disappointed to see that no pane of the window was big enough for my body to pass through. Out there I would be covered with warmth and softness. I could lie peacefully under that snow, and no one would find my body until spring. My thoughts raced on — wildly, crazily. I shivered. I couldn't live another hour. Not another minute. I bit my lips and dug my nails into the palms of my hands until they bled. *God, if you're there, hear me,* I begged. *I can't take this. I'm exhausted. My body has no strength, and I have no hope.*

Then my legs collapsed and my arms went limp. My head floated. I stumbled back to bed, and soon after a nurse came into my room and gave me a sedative. I awoke later; I was still alive.

This was far from the last time I thought about suicide, but I never again longed for it with such intensity.

Woman's "Role"?

In thy wife thou {husband} shalt have gladness,
she shall fill thy home with good,
happy in her loving service
and the joys of motherhood.

"Blest the Man That Fears Jehovah,"
stanza 2

EARLY ONE MORNING in February, my doctor and a nurse came into my room. Next, two young men in white wheeled in a black box with wires and "head receivers" attached. Pain streaked through my stomach. In a minute my head would explode. "What are you going to do?" I asked.

My doctor sat on my bed, took my hand, and said, "We're starting a few shock [electroconvulsive] treatments," he said. "They don't hurt. You won't even know you're getting a treatment, and it will be over in a few seconds. I think these will help with your depression. Trust me."

My body shook. My mouth was dry. My doctor stayed as

one of the assistants attached the wires to my head. We patients called it "wiring."

I woke up much later. I liked the dreamless sleep because for that two or three hours I didn't have to think. I hadn't felt the shock; I remembered only the fear. No one told me how many treatments I would need, but a pattern developed: I usually got a treatment on Monday, Wednesday, and Friday. On these days my first thought in the morning was, Will I or won't I get a treatment today? Each time I was anxious, even though the treatments were painless.

Physically painless, yes — but not without troublesome aftereffects. My doctor always visited me the day after a treatment, but he never assured me that I had had the last one. When he asked how I felt, I would cry. Sometimes I was confused, sometimes sad; at other times my mind was blank. Because of their unpredictable effects, shock treatments not only frightened me; they humiliated and angered me.

For some patients, my doctor told me, electroconvulsive therapy was necessary. (I was convinced that talk therapy helped me more.) When I was very agitated, the treatments may have helped. I don't know; my doctor said they did. But they didn't bring long periods of relief, and I was still obsessed by my guilt. (Electroconvulsive therapy fell into disfavor for a time. Then, during the mid-1980s, it was again used as an effective therapy for clinical depression.)

In any case, my doctor continued the shock treatments. (These were the first of several series of treatments I would receive during the next several years.) Later on, the hospital provided a special room for that purpose. I was given a muscle relaxant to soften the seizure; they told me it would prevent me from thrashing around and possibly breaking a bone. A doctor also injected a quick-acting anesthetic that I appreciated. I was still anxious but not afraid.

But I remained dissatisfied with some of the effects of the treatments. I complained to my doctor that they didn't help me forget the pain of being *me,* and they erased any good recent memories I may have had. Even today I have no memory of a sizeable part of my children's young lives. I don't know, however, if that's a result of the many shock treatments or of the sickness itself.

The memories I did have were so painful. Weren't shock treatments supposed to help? I asked my doctor at my next therapy session. He didn't answer but instead hinted that my problems ran deep and that the difficulties Ray and I had had in Nigeria were not the cause. Nigeria was merely the circumstance, the occasion for my present distress, he said. But I didn't believe him, so I told him how I thought my present problems had started.

I began by talking about the children. Both Ray and I had wanted children, I told the doctor. World War II had separated us for three-and-a-half years, and Kenneth, our first child, didn't arrive for another two-and-a-half years after the war ended. We were overjoyed. When I was pregnant with Kenneth, I felt better than at any other time in my life. Even headaches were rare.

Within three years, Ray and I had two more children. Donna arrived on my birthday, the best birthday present I ever got. Never having had a sister, I had always dreamed of having a daughter, and she made my dream come true. Sixteen months later, when Susan came, Ray and I were both happy again — I, especially.

Life was good, and we wanted it to stay that way. Our three children, all very close in age, kept us busy parents, and since we were anticipating going to Africa, it seemed best not to have another child too soon. Ray agreed.

Today I think, Well? What's wrong with that? But at the time I believed that a woman's principal role was to bear and nurture children, and that God gives a woman additional strength with each child. How many times had I not sung these words from "Blest the Man That Fears Jehovah," the hymn based on Psalm 128:

> In thy wife thou {husband} shalt have gladness,
> She shall fill thy home with good,
> Happy in her loving service
> And the joys of motherhood.
> Joyful children, sons and daughters,
> Shall about thy table meet,
> Olive plants, in strength and beauty,
> Full of hope and promise sweet.

I heard it from the pulpit. I heard it from my mother. I believed it, and I felt it. God determines the number of children in a family; mothers do not. Birth control was sin. To decide when and how many children to have was the height of arrogance. Those decisions belonged to God. So the monthly relief I felt when I knew I wasn't pregnant was not as great as the pain that seared my conscience about the sin of practicing birth control. Finally, after Ray and I had been in Lupwe for over a year, I couldn't bear the guilt anymore, and Ray and I stopped the practice. The next month I was pregnant. Ken was five and a half when Anita was born.

When the first few months of nausea were past and I felt life within me, I was peaceful and quietly happy. But not for long. A gnawing anxiety replaced the guilt I had felt earlier. Fatigue, depression, and an inability to do my ordinary "work" overcame me. In addition, I worried that my baby would not be born well. I knew God was just, and he knew I had sinned, so I was afraid that something would be wrong with my baby, that my daughter would suffer because of my sin. I knew, of course, that God is merciful, but at this point I was already beginning to succumb to the sickness that would return us to the States and put me in the hospital. If my child would be born flawed, I kept thinking, it would be my fault.

Toward the end of the eighth month of my pregnancy, the missionary nurse, Anita Vissia, suggested that we travel to Jos (350 miles away, where the hospital was located) and discuss my pregnancy and growing anxiety with the British doctor there. Ray and I and the three little ones traveled part of the way in the Bedford, the mission's rough-riding English truck. But it was too much for me. So we went to the nearest airport, in Makurdi (about 80 miles away), where I boarded a plane. Ray and the three children continued on in the truck.

Since it was a two-seater plane, I sat next to the pilot, a Nigerian who knew very little English. I didn't care; I didn't want to talk anyway. *God, will my baby be dead or alive? Well or deformed?* I remembered a wall hanging that said, "Cast your cares on Me." But I couldn't. Each worry and self-recrimination bounced back, each time with greater force. I turned my head so the pilot wouldn't see me cry.

When the plane arrived in Jos, I went directly to the hospital. It was a Friday. On Monday morning the doctor gave me something to quiet my acrobatic nerves. After a day and a half on castor oil, which was intended to hasten my labor, I was given an injection. Another day went by. I became convinced that I would leave the hospital with empty arms and heart. I didn't have enough energy to cooperate much. Mercifully, one more injection helped me give birth to my daughter.

My fourth child was born on Wednesday, May 6, 1953, a perfectly formed baby. When I held her close, I felt how deeply I loved her. We named her Anita — after Anita Vissia, who was my role model, a woman whose Christian maturity I would never attain.

I thanked God for my baby. But laughter and joy didn't replace my tears — in fact, I began crying more and more.

After telling my doctor about this part of my life, I felt better, but I was exhausted. I thought of my baby, now in the home of good friends John and Jean VanderVeen, who were loving and caring for her far better than I had during her first six months in Nigeria. Maybe this was my punishment — not being able to take care of my own children. Perhaps I would never get my children back again. But I was too tired to care.

My doctor kept me in his office until I pulled myself together. After this exchange, he changed his diagnosis:

> This patient is probably [experiencing] a psychotic depressive reaction. I had hoped that the diagnosis could be placed under the psychoneurotic disorder with the diagnosis of depressive reaction, but her preoccupation, agitation, sleeplessness, and the severity of her guilt feelings with the history of psychomotor retardation and rather profound retardation of thought at times, throws the weight of evidence, at the present time, into the psychotic depressive group. Furthermore, there is a factor of the birth of a baby on May 6 plus consideration of her personality makeup before the present episode.

I could not see how anyone could call my problems "sickness." My problem was sin, guilt, and rejection by God. I tried daily to find some comfort — any kind of comfort — in my Bible. What little I did manage to absorb from it was entirely accusatory and made me feel more wretched. I told my doctor.

"Put your Bible away," he said. "You aren't able to read it right just now."

I threw it into my dresser drawer, feeling a bit relieved but even more guilty. Still, I knew I was too tired to try to find the answers myself. I needed someone with spiritual insight to help me.

Maybe my pastor could help.

Mercy

O my soul, why are you grieving,
why disquieted in me?
Put your hope in God, believing
he will still your refuge be.

"As a Deer in Want
of Water," stanza 3
(Psalm 42)

MY BOUT with contemplated suicide and the shock treatments left me even weaker than before. Now and then the confusion lifted, but never enough for me to think logically and clearly.

I had put my Bible aside, but that didn't mean I could easily set aside the texts, commands, and judgments that I had learned from the Bible, my ministers, my Christian teachers, and my parents. God had said, "No testing has overtaken you that is not common to everyone. God is faithful, and he will not let you be tested beyond your strength" (1 Cor. 10:13,

NRSV). But wasn't I burdened beyond my ability to cope? Hopelessness filled the core of my body.

Questions churned in my head. Why do I feel so guilty? Why have I gone so wrong? What is guilt, anyway? Christians have rules based on the Bible, and when you break them, you're guilty, and you feel guilty. Are guilt feelings good for Christians? Is there such a thing as imitation guilt? How can I tell if my guilt is real or not? I can't even think straight, so how will I ever think clearly about this?

Whatever guilt I was suffering from didn't let up. I wanted to be purged not only of this guilt but also of my anger against people who had hurt me. Any kind of punishment would be better than my self-inflicted torture. A punishment decided by others, I reasoned, would at least come to an end at some point.

Although my doctor had suggested I stop reading the Bible for awhile, I thought my pastor, the Reverend Henry DeMots (now retired), might be able to help me, and Ray agreed. Reverend DeMots had visited me several times, and I appreciated him even though my childhood memories of ministers were colored dark by my anguish. (If ministers measure the success of their sermons by how guilty they make their listeners feel, then I had heard many successful ministers in my youth.)

I looked forward to my pastor's visits because he neither judged nor condemned me. Always gentle, sincere, and quiet, he empathized with whatever feelings I shared with him. He understood me and what I was talking about. He understood why my doctor had suggested I put away my Bible for awhile.

He also understood my obsession with sin and guilt and didn't recite scores of texts to try to prove me wrong. He saw how I would isolate a text, especially one that accused or condemned me, and apply it absolutely.

When he stopped by at my request, we talked about prayer. I told him I couldn't pray. I explained that I was having a very hard time overcoming my anger about some of the problems Ray and I had had on the mission field.

"It's all right for you not to pray for a while," he said, to my shocked surprise. "That's what other Christians are for: they can do your praying for you."

"*Other Christians,* yes," I said, "but I'm not an *other Christian.* I can't forgive people, so God won't forgive me. Doesn't the Bible say, 'If you do not forgive men their sins, your Father will not forgive your sins'? So it won't help for others to pray for me."

"You're forgetting one thing: you're judging yourself and can't forgive yourself. God judges you, true. The difference is that God has mercy, and you have none for yourself. You're forgetting that God understands us, even when we don't understand ourselves, him, or his Word. He has mercy, enough for every situation and every person. He pardons generously and freely.

"Sometimes when we can't pray," he continued, "we can repeat certain words of prayer. Would you be willing to repeat certain words after me?"

I agreed. He began slowly: "Our Father who art in heaven . . ." I repeated the words. "Hallowed be thy Name . . ." Again I repeated the words. We continued together until we came to the words "as we forgive our debtors." A tortured sob escaped my lips: "No, I can't. I can't."

Reverend DeMots stopped praying, stood up, and gently placed his hand on my shoulder. If he was shocked, he didn't show it. He said nothing.

"How can I ever forgive myself for botching things up this way — our work, my family, everything?"

"I don't know how just now," he said, "but I do know this: God is still in control."

"But there are lots of people whose lives are much tougher than mine and who have done much worse in life than I have, and they don't fall apart when things go wrong. Some aren't even Christians, and they do just fine. Look at me: I can't eat, I can't walk without shaking, and I'm dead tired. I can't forgive all that."

He explained to me that all God's children are flawed and do make mistakes — which I had learned in childhood, of course. But all mistakes aren't sin, he said, and what's more, God protects all those for whom Christ died. (Matthew 5:48 — "Be perfect, therefore, as your heavenly Father is perfect" — ran through my mind, but I kept it to myself.)

"But that's the whole point," I cried. "He's not protecting me. I can't be sure that I'm one of those for whom Christ died. I know that I'm not saved. God has rejected me. In fact, sometimes I wonder if God even exists." I trembled.

"You know, Lillian," Reverend DeMots replied, "you can't really feel God's absence if you've never believed that he existed." He looked at me, not speaking until I had regained some composure.

"Did you ever believe you were one of God's children?" he asked.

"You know I did," I protested. Reverend DeMots had been our minister before Ray and I had left for the mission field, and he knew that I was a serious person — sometimes too serious — always concerned with how much I was (or wasn't) doing for the "advancement of God's kingdom." For Ray and me, church and kingdom "activities" were the center of our lives, and we enjoyed them.

"Well, then," he said, very slowly and very quietly, "what makes you think God changes his mind about his children?"

I couldn't answer. Slowly I soaked up that good news. I knew Reverend DeMots was right. God doesn't disinherit his children, so he hadn't let me go, either. A sliver of light pierced the darkness in my soul. "I never thought of that," I said. "I thought I had committed the unpardonable sin, and that God had rejected me."

My tense and tired body went limp. For the first time since I had been hospitalized, I felt some peace. Never again did I feel that God had damned me, even though I hadn't begun the struggle to build a *joyful* relationship with him.

Reverend DeMots prayed again, not with me this time, but for me. He urged God to draw me to himself because just now I couldn't come on my own. He reminded God of the many prayers that were being said for me and that God had promised always to hear the prayers of people who believed in him. He told God how weary I was and how badly I needed rest. He asked God to help my psychiatrist straighten out my confusion about my guilty *feelings* (not my guilt). And he thanked God for the fine Christian hospital I was in and for the love I was being shown here.

I remember the details of my minister's prayer because it represented a big step for me. I'm not sure that I was praying with him, but I could remember his prayer. I didn't know whether God would answer it.

I continued to cope with feeling sinful and guilty. If I were one of God's children — and now I believed I was — then Cain and Abel were both living within me. I still didn't believe that I was ill. I still thought that if I could rid myself of my guilt, then my spirits would rise. When I felt better, I'd be able to pick up the past where it had left me off — in Nigeria, as a wife and mother and worker in God's kingdom there.

But there is no quick fix for deep depression. I had been in the hospital for nearly six weeks, and I would be there quite a bit longer.

The King's Business

. . . troubles now surround my life,
my sins have overtaken me.
They overwhelm my failing heart;
I cannot see, my way is dark.
Be pleased, O Lord, to rescue me;
come quickly and restore my life.

Bert Polman, "I Waited Patiently
for God," stanza 3
(Psalm 40)

MY MINISTER kept reassuring me that I was one of God's children, but I still had many doubts. My faith, rather than relieving my depression, intensified it. I knew the *facts* of Christianity, but I didn't trust them. My faith was so badly damaged that I still had trouble trusting my doctor.

A cascade of thoughts and feelings continued to overwhelm me. Why am I unable to be on the mission field? Why am I so afraid to meet people? Why am I afraid? Why do I feel so worthless? I was desperate for answers. I had learned years ago that faith unlived is unreal. Life becomes worthwhile and challenging when faith is lived. Maybe that was the answer to these troublesome questions: I wasn't living my faith.

I had been raised in the stern tradition and with the sometimes narrow biblical interpretations of John Calvin. I believe, as I was taught, that all of life is religion. As a sign I saw once in front of a church put it, "If Christ isn't Lord of all, then he isn't Lord at all." We journey from birth to heaven, and we serve him as we travel. No area or time of life can be separated from our main purpose: to serve God. And yet, I had been trying to live this way (or so I thought), and my world had come crashing down with me pinned underneath it.

Yes, I knew that anything we do to serve *self* has no importance in God's sight. So I reasoned that I'd been sent home from Nigeria in disgrace because too much of my *self* had been hampering the work of God's kingdom there.

I had missed the obvious: if all of life is religion and is to be used to further God's kingdom, then maintaining a home and raising children — who also belong to God — is an important kingdom activity. I loved my family, but I had continued to look for purposeful work I could do for God *in addition to* caring for my family. I had been overambitious and stupid, and now God was teaching me something, wasn't he, by taking my family away from me? What did God want from me?

Why was God keeping me from making sense out of life? If I knew, I wouldn't have to be in this hospital, and I could get about my — his — business! Christ said, "If you have faith as small as a mustard seed . . . nothing will be impossible for you" (Matt. 17:20). Obviously, my faith was even smaller.

Later, my minister explained that although our faith may be weak, the Lord's love is not. He had raised Jairus's daughter from the dead and healed an insane man, so emotional sickness wasn't too tough for him. "If change depended on our faith," my pastor said, "we would be taking credit for it rather than giving it to God."

I tried to remember and believe what he said, but I still struggled. I was tortured by a pronouncement someone had made: "If only you were right with the Lord, this wouldn't happen." How had I become so "wrong with the Lord"? Again and again I reviewed the last few years of my life. Had going to Africa with three little children been wrong, as some had suggested? Had I gone to serve self instead of God?

My doctor's hint that going to Nigeria had not caused my illness rankled. He pointed out the difference between *being* guilty and *feeling* guilty. "They're not the same, you know. Sometimes feeling guilty is a way of saying, 'I'm inferior.'" I thought of many ways in which I was inferior: I was a poor wife and mother, I was a failure as a missionary, I had few talents, I didn't know how to get along with people — my list was long. And now another troublesome thought introduced itself: Were my feelings of inferiority somehow related to my never having gone to college? Becoming a teacher had been my childhood dream — until that dream was dashed in the tenth grade. My mother believed that only boys needed a college education. Girls, she said, had to learn how to cook, sew, keep house, care for a husband, and raise children. It had hurt to lose my dream, but I didn't see how my lack of education could relate to my present situation.

My doctor made these comments in his record of my treatment:

> She says that she has waves of a feeling that she must always do more for the Kingdom than what she was doing all of her life. She recognizes that the work that she was actually doing on the mission field was not more, and, in

fact, not as much of a load as she had frequently carried before. She also recognizes . . . that for the first year and a half she did not have this kind of difficulty, but that it came on . . . her during the last few months of her stay there. . . .

Patient [also] goes into some detail about the frustration she has in not going to college and [I suggest it may be related to] her constant urge to do something more than she can do by only caring for her husband and children. [She is] beginning to realize this but finds it hard to be satisfied, as yet, with this alone.

My ideas — about not having a college education, not understanding the extent to which raising children is a kingdom activity, and not doing enough for God's kingdom — began to move closer together, but still I couldn't connect them.

Even though I repeated myself frequently, my doctor remained patient, trying to help me with the connections. He recorded these notes after one of our sessions:

The patient has been seen several times, but not much has come from the interviews. . . . Today she is somewhat petulant and downhearted and states that she feels that she is going backward. One of the reasons for this is that she feels that if she has headaches because she didn't go to college, then she is also striving for something that she can't achieve and can't accept the fact that she can't achieve it, and therefore is responsible for her actions.

This woman has misunderstood and misinterpreted things. She usually does not do this, but apparently there was something in talking about the college situation which has caused her a considerable amount of difficulty since, as she now states, she has been frequently consciously aware of the fact that she hasn't had a college education and has secretly hoped that she could attend college. She says that when she left for Africa she felt that now she could do something on the level of individuals who have gone to college, even though she herself has not. She thinks that this was wrong and [that this way of perceiving it] made it a sin, and she is now paying for this sinful act.

This woman is very depressed today. She cries sometimes during the interview. The situation is straightened out as far as her misunderstanding and misinterpretation is concerned. It is quite evident that one has to be very careful what one says to this individual, as she is a very meticulous person and must always interpret things and remember things exactly as they are, and if she cannot remember them and interpret them, then she is uneasy. If she interprets them wrongly [she usually does so in a way that involves] self-deprecation and self-accusation.

She appears to be somewhat better when she leaves the office and the conversation today centers more [on] utilizing those things which we have, rather than striving after something which we do not have, and bringing out the point that individuals with less education can often do more than individuals with a great deal of education. Also the fact that the simple factor of going to college does not make an educated person nor one who knows a good deal nor one with common sense. . . .

After some conversation she realizes that an individual does not have to go to college in order to do something worthwhile in this world. However, she still holds to her idea of having wanted to go to college and to a certain extent blames herself for wanting to do that because that was just self-aggrandizement. To put the matter on an intellectual and logical level, it is quite evident that if a minister or doctor or lawyer or engineer or anyone wanted to go to school beyond high school, then he too must [have done] that for his own self-satisfaction and self-aggrandizement rather than following his instincts and desire to prepare himself for some kind of work, or simply for the sake of learning about something about which he is curious.

She sees the point all right, but it is always difficult for this woman to apply things to herself, especially if they have a ray of hope in them.

As usual, she is very thankful for an interview [I was always polite], and I believe that she should be seen more frequently.

There are many elements which are mixed in this woman. Some of [what she feels] is paranoid. There is a definite feeling of inferiority and a mixture of lack of confidence of self, with an urge and drive to do things, and she does things very well, so there is no need for lack of confidence. This sort of thing is mixed with the fact that she admits frequently that some of the things which she has done have been good, done properly. . . .

She says she never has even talked to her husband about her wanting to go to college, and this has bothered her greatly.

After this session I left my doctor's office somewhat encouraged, and I thought clearly for a little while. Periods like this were very important to my progress.

When I got back to my room, two visitors — distant relatives — were waiting for me. Immediately my serenity fled, and humiliation overwhelmed me. My feelings of shame, defeat, and failure multiplied when anyone came to see me who knew that I had been sent home from Africa. After this episode my doctor gave orders that I was to have no visitors other than Ray and my pastor.

Later Ray came, and we went for a short ride. When we got back to the hospital, I was exhausted. How can anyone get this tired from a short ride? I wondered. I went to bed.

Would morning never end my constant night?

I Can't

My guilt has overwhelmed me. . . .
There is no health in my body.
I am feeble and utterly crushed;
I groan in anguish of heart.

Psalm 38:4, 7, 8

SPRING DID COME. Finally. It was March. The snow was disappearing, and the sun penetrated the dark pines that fronted the building. But my sadness remained. During the gray winter I had wondered whether — if I lived until spring — spring would inspire my weary soul. But my sadness, unlike the snow, did not disappear with the sunshine. I had to accept the fact that winter was not the cause of my depression.

Nights still seemed long, although I was sleeping a little better, and I was getting along on one or two sleeping pills a night. But the days, which were getting longer, seemed eternal. Waking up in the morning meant I would have to live another day. Inside me was an unfocused yearning for what never was and what would never be. Maybe someday my head might have answers about what troubled me, but my heart would always be sad. I still felt worthless.

Although I didn't realize it at the time, this kind of negative self-evaluation is not uncommon among Christians. In *The Christian Looks at Himself,* Anthony Hoekema comments, "It would seem that people who accept the Christian view of man as a creature made in God's image and redeemed from sin by the sacrifice of God's own Son would have, for the most part, a very positive self-image. Unfortunately, however, this is by no means the case. Conservative evangelical Christians often have a rather negative self-image."

Dr. Hoekema must have sung from the same songbook I did, because he goes on to make this observation:

> Some of the hymns of the church have made their contribution to the negative self-image often found among Christians. In my younger days we used to sing a version of the hymn "Beneath the Cross of Jesus" which went like this, in the second stanza:
>
> > *And from my smitten heart with tears,*
> > *Two wonders I confess:*
> > *The wonders of his glorious love*
> > *And my own worthlessness.*

He noted that some churches eventually changed "worthlessness" to "unworthiness." But I hadn't reached that point yet.

I was constantly torn by contradictory feelings. I was afraid to be alone, but I was also afraid to be with people. Sometimes I was less lonely when I was by myself than when I was with my husband. Yet I always needed him.

Guilt is so possessive. It clutches every waking moment.

My brain, which felt shredded, had no logical power to work against my illogical thoughts. Certain words and phrases cut grooves in my brain that imprisoned me. I was haunted by self-accusations: *I brought all of this on myself. I'll never get better. I can't do anything well. I'm a terrible wife and mother. It's my fault we're not in Nigeria.* "She's like a broken record," Ray often said to friends. "Like a needle caught in a record groove, she repeats the same thoughts and ideas. They don't fade. They don't wear out." But he always listened patiently.

In *The Christian's Handbook of Psychiatry,* O. Quentin Hyder writes perceptively about guilt:

> [It] is a mixture of many emotions and thoughts which destroy inner peace. It is partly the unpleasant knowledge that something wrong has been done. It is partly fear of punishment. It is shame, regret, or remorse. . . . It leads to loneliness and isolation . . . It is partly depression and partly anxiety. It is partly true and [partly] false. . . .
>
> In the case of false guilt there is the erroneous belief that there exists that separation [from God] even though that is not actually the situation. . . .
>
> Self-hatred is an element here and this leads to great difficulty in accepting forgiveness.

Guilt is so hard to get rid of and so easily fueled. Like the burning bush that Moses saw in the wilderness, it burns — but the voice of God is not in it. It feeds on itself, or others feed it by suggesting that God would come to your aid if you were guiltless. "If you are pure and upright," Bildad the Shuhite said to Job, "even now [God] will rouse himself on your behalf" (8:6). Stoked this way, the fire burns hotter.

Despite this turmoil, my next session with my doctor began more calmly. But I was still repeating the same things over and over. I could not be persuaded that the experience Ray and I had had in Nigeria had not caused my present "condition." By this time I was convinced that we would never go back. I felt guilty that the world missions board of our denomination had invested so much in our family and that we had served only two years. I wanted a magic switch to cast a flood of light on my problems.

Would I have a problem being diagnosed with an illness such as cancer, diabetes, or tuberculosis, my doctor asked me. No, I answered, but people *know* those are illnesses. Did I care what "other people" thought? No. Yes. Of course I cared. On the other hand, at this point I didn't want to see "other people" at all.

As long as I believed my situation was sin and not sickness, I could not help myself. God didn't seem to be helping much, either.

My doctor knew I was misperceiving my problem. Over several sessions he gradually tried to help me see that I was ill, and that my illness had no quick or easy cure. "Penicillin can erase a fever in twenty-four to forty-eight hours," he said, "but the patient doesn't become well right away, so the penicillin isn't discontinued. Depression is more difficult to cure because the causes aren't immediately obvious. And even when the causes are finally recognized, the patient must learn how to deal with them."

Meanwhile, I had to live with my regrets — and one of my biggest regrets was that my family was split up because I wasn't behaving as a Christian mother and homemaker would. I was running — no, crawling — in demonic circles. Whenever I had an idea that began to help me accept that I was ill with depression, it was immediately attacked by my feelings of worthlessness. I was stuck; I wasn't moving forward a bit.

After one of these sessions in which my doctor and I discussed depression as an illness, he made these notes:

She still interprets all this to mean that she brought this on herself and that she is responsible for it. She says that she cannot accept it as an illness but that it is rather an act of will.

She is resting a great deal better and is sleeping better at night although she still uses one or sometimes two sleeping tablets. She says that she feels at ease as long as she is in the hospital but feels uneasy when she is out of the hospital if she thinks she might meet someone whom she might know. She does not as yet see that the basis for her depression [can be] reasons over which she herself could not have had control.

In general her ideas are changing somewhat but she is adamant in some of them up to this point. . . . She begins to show signs of having some insight, in spite of the fact that she mentions that she still cannot see this as an illness. Another interview will be held with her tomorrow in an effort to determine just what course it is that one should proceed to take here.

The next day my doctor and I talked again. The session was very troubling to me because he suggested that certain events in my childhood might have precipitated my depression. I didn't believe him. I clasped my hands so tightly they hurt, and I bit my lip until it bled. I insisted that my depression was the result of my inability to handle the Nigerian situation in a Christian way, and that I would have to clear this up before I could look for other reasons.

"Think about what I've said," he replied. "We don't always know what *causes* sickness, and we keep trying to find out. We don't know much about what causes cancer, for example, so we keep looking. But we do know many things that can cause depression, and perhaps you and I could explore them together."

I shook my head. "That's not a fair comparison. Cancer is physical. This is between my ears. I should be able to exercise self-discipline and get over it."

"Maybe," he replied, "but it would help to know a little more about your life before Nigeria." When he said that I thought of my mother and her teaching: telling the truth was always easier because it wouldn't trip you up afterward. Not that I believed her. It's not easy to tell the truth all the time. So my doctor's encouraging me to be truthful with and about myself was a challenge.

Questions raced through my head. If I tell myself the lie that I could do anything if I only had the chance, who suffers? If I tell myself the lie that I can't do anything because I don't have the chance, who suffers? If I tell myself the lie that everything's fine with me, my home, my family, that everything is completely successful, completely in hand, and well-balanced, who suffers?

My mind was in high gear again, and my doctor and I went nowhere at a dizzying speed.

It seemed to me that this session just made things worse. But when I got back to my room, I did start to think about the past: my childhood, school, my brothers, my parents, work, my marriage, World War II, and more. Event after event flitted through my mind like frames from an old movie. Then some old *feelings* — vague and unhappy — began to take shape. I started to cry uncontrollably. The nurse came in and calmed me down with a sedative.

I didn't want to think about the past. The pain of those memories was intense, the despair deeper.

But it was necessary pain, I slowly began to realize. I would have to lay bare the sources of my negative feelings — if I could identify them — before my depression could lift. For too long I had been in the habit of shoving unwanted emotions into a closet and locking the door. Now I would need help to open that door. I would need help to look at my makeup, my childhood, my family, and my experiences and to figure out, if possible, how I had become Case No. 5352 in a mental hospital.

Finally I understood. I was sick. Very sick.

I didn't know the prognosis, nor did I know then how agonizing my search would be.

The Girl with the Curl

Even a child is known by {her} actions.

Proverbs 20:11

Folly is bound up in the heart of a child.

Proverbs 22:15

IT WAS NOW April. As the days crawled on, it became less real to me that I was indeed very ill mentally and emotionally. But the symptoms continued, and I couldn't think clearly. I was hopeless. When my helplessness matched my despair, I looked back on my childhood. Because most of my thoughts were flighty, sketchy, and muddled, I wrote down what clear thoughts I had and took the notes with me the next time I had a session with my doctor.

I had been born thirty-one years earlier to Dutch Calvinist parents who were immigrants. My parents' values were shaped by their beliefs. They believed that all Christian life fitted into the box of their belief system, which had been shaped during their youth in the Netherlands. And they protected their children from anything that did not fit in that box.

The girl I remembered was chubby and chunky. Her hair when her mother curled it didn't fit well with a tomboy's delights and temperament. She had round cheeks that reddened easily, both in play and in embarrassment. She had straight eyebrows, an easy, friendly smile, and a jutting lower lip that accentuated her frequent displeasure or moodiness. She had a hard fist that could match the power of her brothers', if she needed to use it. And occasionally she did.

I was energetic, ambitious, persistent, and often rebellious. I was jealous of my brothers (they got to do lots of things that girls weren't allowed to do) and sensitive to their frequent teasing (although I teased them too). Usually I was noisy and busy, but when I wasn't "busy," as well as when I was moody, I very often would read. I enjoyed being alone as much as I liked being with other people. (Looking back, I wonder: If my parents had taken me to a psychiatrist when I was a child, would my moodiness have been diagnosed as depression?)

As a child I sometimes thought of myself as the girl in one of my nursery-rhyme books:

> There was a little girl
> Who had a little curl
> Right in the middle of her forehead.
> And when she was good,
> She was very, very good,
> But when she was bad she was horrid.

God knows I tried to be a good girl; I prayed to him enough about it. Sometimes I prayed while I was being punished. But the gulf between God and me was wide; my prayers seldom seemed to span it.

Sometimes I thought that prayer didn't help anything, not as far as I could see, anyway. Often I asked God to help me be good, but he never seemed to respond. Very early in school I learned Matthew 7:7: "Ask and it will be given to you; seek and you will find; knock and the door will be opened to you." I asked, I sought, and I knocked, but I received no answers, I found nothing, and no one answered the door. I often thought I just wasn't good enough to have God answer my prayers. After all, I did disobey my mother, and I did get very angry with her. Sometimes I didn't even *want* to be good.

At other times, usually at night when I went to bed, I asked God to forgive me just once more. Maybe he did, but I never felt forgiven, either by him or by my mother. Things got mixed up. I hoped heaven would be different than my childhood.

My parents had five children: four boys and a girl — me. Bernie, my older brother, was born in the Netherlands. Since my parents emigrated shortly after that, I and my three younger brothers — Gerry, Frank, and Henry — were born in America, in Michigan.

Pa was a baked-goods peddler, and we lived in a very modest blue-collar neighborhood in Grand Rapids. During the Great Depression, we were very poor. As in most Dutch Calvinist families, the two most important things in our family were the church and the Christian school.

The Leonard Refrigerator Company (later the Kelvinator plant), built in 1911, provided employment to most of the men in the neighborhood. The factory ran along one street, and we lived on London Street, one of the seven blocks that intersected it, forming perpendicular rows of workers' houses. Ma warned me about all those men "at the end of the street" and ordered me straight home from school.

Ma ran the house; that was her role. I helped Ma a lot, not because I was a nice girl but because I was the only girl she had. She was always telling me what to do. Set the table. Dry the dishes. Sweep the front porch. Make your bed. Empty the water under the icebox, and don't spill it. Polish your shoes — and everybody else's (that was Saturday's instruction). Take care of your little brothers. Put this away. Put that away. I was Ma's chief assistant, and she kept me busy because she couldn't stand a mess: company might drop in.

Some of my memories of childhood are warm and positive. Those memories involve not only books and school but also our attic in the house on London Street where we lived until I was twelve. Sometimes the house and the family didn't seem like home to me. I lived at our house, of course, and I didn't want to be anywhere else, sure, but my *home* was the attic.

I loved the attic because it was mine. The boys wanted no part of it, at least when I was up there. I was comfortable there. Even the somberness of the long shadows cast by the single dim bulb added to the warmth I felt. It was the only place I could be alone with my doll family. I spent many wonderful hours playing with them — an activity Ma approved of. She let me use all the scraps of cotton, wool, and silk left over from her sewing to make doll clothes. There were also ribbons, buttons, lace, and even, I remember, a small piece of fur.

What Ma didn't know was that I never played "house." I played "school." My pupils were very well dressed. They loved their teacher, and their teacher loved them. I read to them, sang to them, and taught them what I had learned in school.

One especially tender memory stands out in my mind. It was raining fiercely that day I was in the attic. Thunder and lightning seemed to be just above the eaves. Suddenly I heard a terrifying clap, and a vivid light filled the attic near the spot where I was playing.

I was scared — and alone. But just then I heard Ma running up the stairs shouting, *"Meisje, meisje, are you all right?"* She rushed through the doorway, grabbed me, and held me close. My fear left as quickly as it had come; I felt warm and safe with her arms around me.

But most of my childhood memories aren't so pleasant. Many remind me of the different kinds of treatment my brothers and I got — even "small" memories like cookie-weighing. Because Pa was a baked-goods peddler, he kept bulk cookies in the basement. We children often weighed the cookies into one-pound bags. Ma insisted that we sing or whistle as we weighed, because she knew we couldn't eat cookies and sing or whistle at the same time. I became a good whistler, but the only time I was allowed to whistle — unlike my brothers — was during cookie-weighing time. Girls don't whistle, my mother told me.

Sometimes I can't understand why my brothers say they have few bad memories of childhood. Some of the stories they recall with gales of laughter make me cringe, and others that they dismiss with a shrug of the shoulders are painful to me. Were my memories different because they were boys and I was the only girl? (When I was much older, a friend said to me, "Never forget that in all communication there is a sending set, a receiving set, and a message. If any part isn't functioning right, the message will be garbled." My receiving set may have malfunctioned since my birth.)

I learned early that the difference between boys and girls is huge. I first learned this lesson when we played games. I loved to play games, any kind, the more competitive the better. But girls didn't play all kinds of games, Ma told me; some games were for boys, and some were for girls. Take mumblety-peg, for example. You need a jackknife to play that, and girls don't *play* with knives. Girls, Ma said, *use* knives. I managed to learn to play in spite of her injunction, and I beat the boys once in a while.

Playing marbles "for keeps" wasn't proper for girls, either. Bernie had a box with a zillion marbles, including some beautiful glassies that he had won because of his skill. But when he played with me, I had to return anything I won. Girls, Ma said, play with jacks.

The difference between boys and girls showed up in other ways too. For one thing, my brothers had fewer household chores than I did. They helped with the yard work, although Pa did most of that, because he loved tending flowers and manicuring the lawn. And sometimes the boys washed Pa's truck (he got his first one in 1928). But other than that, they didn't do much around the house. I, on the other hand, was always busy following Ma's orders.

Boys had bicycles with a bar from back to front; they could swing a leg over the bar easily and decently because they wore pants. But at that time, girls needed a bar-less two-wheeler to accommodate the skirts they wore. In our family there was only enough money for one bike, so we got a "boys' bike." That meant my brothers could ride it and I couldn't.

The list of things I couldn't do seemed endless. Boys could swing on the bars at school, but they didn't want to. I wanted to do it, but it was improper because my panties would show. (Girls always wore dresses; slacks and shorts for girls hadn't been introduced yet.) Boys could play outdoors after supper even after the streetlights went on. I had to go inside. Boys combed their hair in a few seconds and didn't care if the part was crooked. I had to stand still to get my hair curled (and my ears burned) with a curling iron. Otherwise, Ma explained, people would think she wasn't a good mother.

These were among the memories that I wrote down and subsequently discussed with my doctor. I began to see, as he and I talked, what an extremely sensitive child I had been. I also saw that maybe some of my aggressive boisterousness had been a coverup for that sensitivity.

A couple of my teachers must have recognized this. My seventh-grade math teacher had tried to help me see myself more clearly. "You," he said, "are like a turtle with a hard shell. You hide your real self under a hard, impenetrable shell of noise. Inside is a gentle and sensitive person. Once in a while the real you comes out, slowly, carefully, but if someone hurts your feelings just a little, you pop inside."

My eighth-grade history and Bible teacher had said, "Your behavior doesn't allow anyone to see the real you." She suggested that she and I study the "Christlike way" together. So every Monday afternoon, week after week, she spent from half an hour to an hour with me after school. Carefully she explained the Sermon on the Mount, and she required me to learn a section of it every week. I learned the passages well; she was proud and so was I. When I remembered to practice what I was learning, I was less noisy and more ladylike. But more often the passages accused me, especially Matthew 5:48: "Be perfect, therefore, as your heavenly Father is perfect." I had stumbled over those words ever since eighth grade, and they disturbed my conscience continually. So did the words my science teacher had tacked above the chalkboard at the front of the classroom. In black poster-paper letters that were ten inches high was the assertion FORGETTING IS SIN. It had a chilling effect.

Still, most of my memories of school are good ones. In high school I enjoyed all my subjects. But even though I liked being in school, I took a big course load every semester so that I could graduate in less than the usual four years and get into the work world earlier. In addition, my parents insisted that I pay my own tuition, because the Depression had hit them hard.

I don't recall that it drew our family together. Now I understand better what happened to my parents and why money was so important, but at the time I viewed the Depression as one big nuisance. For my parents it was far more than that. When Pa missed just one payment on our house, the builder, a fellow Christian who held Pa's land contract, reclaimed it.

When you were poor, your poverty followed you to school. John J. Timmerman taught English in the Christian high school I attended. In *Through a Glass Lightly,* he writes that in 1938 "there was only a tinge of cliquishness in the school: the affluent students were few, and most students were sacrificially supported by their parents or by their hard-earned money." I was one of those students who had to pay her own way with her own "hard-earned" money — which I made by working 15-20 hours a week in a bakery. I participated in as many extracurricular activities as I could, but I never felt like part of the "in" group. I was from the "wrong side of the tracks," both literally and socially. I felt unpopular and inferior, even among my four best friends.

I'm sure that Dr. Timmerman speaks the truth and that my much different recollection says more about me than about the facts. But there were cliques in the school, and they followed mainly economic lines. Girls who wore different colored cashmere sweaters on different days hung out together. Girls who sported too-big sweaters with the big orange C always sat together at games — a distinguished group. During lunch hour, students who had money filled the drugstore near school. Students who came from the wrong quadrants of the city felt the pain of being outsiders.

It took two long sessions for me to tell my doctor this part of my story. What's the good of telling you all this, I asked him bitterly. My words came in spurts — some with tears, all with pain. Both sessions exhausted me, and I spent several sleepless nights after each one. Mainly my doctor listened as I talked, but he made one observation that hit a tender spot. "It seems to me," he said, "that your mother has played quite a role in your life."

I flared up. "My mother was in the United States when this happened," I said vehemently. "I was in Africa — several thousand miles away. How could she possibly have had anything to do with it?"

"I don't know," he said calmly.

After waiting for my heaving sobs to subside, I left his office deeply troubled, my head throbbing. I didn't see how this had anything to do with my failure.

Still, it was food for thought.

Lost Weekend

If I had wings, I'd fly away into the wilderness
to find a quiet, sheltered place where
I could be at rest.

> Helen Otte, "I Need Your Help,
> O Lord My God," stanza 2
> (Psalm 55)

IT SEEMED LIKE a long time before I saw my doctor again (it was actually a week and a half), and I was very depressed. I was mired in thirty years of weed growth in a neglected garden. I felt as though it were Judgment Day. I stood before Lord God Almighty, who saw only the weeds. There was no room for positive thoughts. Hadn't Ma said to me again and again, "Don't forget, *meit* [girl], you must answer for it yourself"?

No, Ma. I didn't forget.

I hadn't seen Ray for several days, because he was attending an institute out of town to update his knowledge and expertise in his trade — installing and repairing air-conditioning and heating systems. This training seemed to say to me that we could not return to the mission field, and I despaired — Africa didn't need furnaces, and no one there had air conditioning.

My doctor couldn't see me just then, so a nurse brought me a sedative, and I fell into a restless sleep. In a dream I saw my children, all much older than the little ones I had abandoned. They didn't know me and refused to come to me. In horror I asked someone, "Where's my baby?" No one answered me. I awoke alone.

Occasionally I asked Ray about the children, but the fact that they were well taken care of and apparently happy pierced my heart. They don't need me either, I concluded.

I longed for my husband. Yet seldom during these wretched months did I concern myself with his well-being. My thoughts centered on me, and even though I was sick and tired of them, I couldn't escape them. That's one of the miseries of depression that people unfamiliar with it can't understand. Meaning well, they say, "Forget about yourself." Oh, God! If I only could!

In April my doctor began to give me passes and allowed me to leave the hospital on Saturday afternoons and evenings. My first time out scared me. It was comfortable, in a perverse way, to be in the hospital. Here I had no responsibility to my husband or my children. I didn't have to think about meals, laundry, or shopping. During my second time out, I became so distressed that I went back to the hospital around 7 p.m. and went to bed.

Now I had been issued my third pass, an overnight pass, but I didn't want it. I was in the pit of depression. But Ray, back from his training, persuaded me. He had arranged for me to see the children. Unfortunately, I didn't want to see them. My dream had scared me.

I don't remember the weekend well, but my doctor recorded Ray's report to him:

On Saturday evening she was lying on the davenport listening to the radio. She became progressively more restless and then she began to mumble and finally she began to say, over and over, "You do not understand it." Between times she seemed to be staring into space and did not respond to his questions. She then started to call the nurse, and [he thought she was] thinking that she was in the hospital. He persuaded her to take some coffee, which she sat up to do. Previous to this time she had been shaking. He says he has seen her shake like this before — during the times she went to the hospital to give birth to one of the children — but the shaking had not been so severe. He then persuaded her to take a warm bath and go to bed. She said that it wasn't time to go to bed but she did do as he suggested after a bit of persuasion.

The next morning she could not understand why she had not pinned up her hair the night before. She [said she couldn't] remember when she hadn't pinned up her hair and asked her husband if he knew whether something had happened to her. She could remember nothing.

He says that she feels relaxed and most at ease when she is with him or when she is in the hospital. He notices that she is beginning to lose her feelings of being at ease when she is with her own family as well as when she is with his family. He now thinks that it was not a good idea for him to go away for a week. He feels she is very dependent on him. This is true but I doubt that his going out of the city for a few days is causative in this instance.

She told him today that she has the feeling that she is not getting better, which is the same feeling she has had periodically between episodes of feeling that she was making some gain.

In the margin of his notes, my doctor had written this comment: "regarding *spell,* probable hysteria."

After this overnight visit, I returned to the hospital overwrought. When I had seen the children, they had greeted me and then returned quickly to their play. That had hurt.

I would soon be insane, I knew. My appetite, which had returned somewhat, disappeared. In a way I knew why I was feeling so wretched. I couldn't erase my doctor's suggestion that my mother "had played quite a role" in my life. Although I had loudly denied that, the possibility haunted me. It had upset me terribly, but I had no idea why. I wondered if it was related to the anxiety I had experienced when I visited my parents briefly on the previous three weekends.

Now I was convinced that I would have to talk to my doctor about my mother. But could any daughter talk about her Christian mother? Could a daughter, one who claimed to be a Christian, be any more disloyal than that? What about God's fifth commandment: Honor your father and your mother?

I hated myself for harboring these thoughts, but I didn't have enough energy to erase them. I was sure they were destroying my mind. Talking might be therapeutic, but maybe I had reached the limits of allowable therapy — at least for a Christian. It was too heavy a responsibility to talk about my mother. In my case, the consequences of this "cure" might be more devastating than the illness. Still, could I be any more of a failure than I already was?

Maybe it would be easier if I talked about my father first. I hadn't said much about him, and my doctor hadn't made any comment about Pa. He wasn't a problem, but I would talk about him anyway.

Pa

Show me your faith without deeds,
and I will show you my faith by what I do.

James 2:18

Pᴀ ᴡᴀs ᴀʙᴏᴜᴛ an inch shorter than Ma and many pounds lighter. He dressed nicely; Ma saw to that. He enjoyed jokes and laughed easily. On Sunday afternoons he took naps, and and when he woke up Ma gave him an orange — a special treat reserved just for him. Oranges were too expensive for children; we had apples. Pa enjoyed cigars, too. Birthdays and Christmases were not complete for him without a box of R. G. Dunns or Dutch Masters. He smoked as we walked to church, and he saved the stub in a diamond-shaped window frame in the church hallway, retrieving it immediately after the service.

Pa also enjoyed opera. I don't think he ever attended one, but he bought recordings of performances. He often whistled the tunes, and I learned to whistle some of them too (only when I was weighing cookies, of course). I still have two of

Pa's recordings, *Tosca* and *Madame Butterfly,* and I cherish them both.

To me he was the best father a girl could have. He delighted in his *kleine meisje* (little girl) and was generous in expressing his delight. Frequently he singled me out for special attention.

He had a horse, Barney, and a wagon he used to peddle his baked goods, and every day he would carefully pack the wagon before he left on his route. My brother Gerry and I sometimes rode old Barney at night when Pa took him to the stall he rented in a barn nearby. When I was about six years old, Pa sold Barney and the wagon and bought a truck. Three days a week his route was in our neighborhood, and the other three days it was in the surrounding rural areas. In the summer, we kids took turns going with him "to the country." We enjoyed it, and I suspect Ma was glad to be free of one of her five children occasionally. Pa always praised me for being a good girl and not begging for cookies, tarts, or rolls.

The Depression years were very bad for Pa's business. We were very poor, and I hated being poor almost as much as I hated being Dutch. Pa continued his route, but often as payment he accepted farm produce or old clothes that Ma would have to restyle for us. Sometimes he gave his customers so much credit that he wouldn't have enough money to pay his weekly bakery bill and still have money left over for the family. This created tension at home. I remember Pa saying, more than once, "Money may not make people happy, but it sure would solve a lot of problems if I had a little more."

Pa loved Ma very much. He loved to tease, and his favorite term of endearment for Ma was *ouwe rook.* Eventually I learned that it means "old crow"; still, Ma enjoyed the pet name. Pa did his best to get her what she wanted, but often his best wasn't enough.

Pa grumbled sometimes, especially when he was hungry. He could become very angry at us or at Ma. But his anger soon melted, and he didn't carry a grudge. He supported Ma in matters of discipline, even though he often didn't agree with her. Often after Ma had punished me, he would try to chase away my tears by saying, "You mustn't take it the way she says it. Take it the way she means it. She means it for your good." But I didn't believe that.

I think they had such different ideas about discipline partly because of the different ways they had come to believe in Jesus Christ. Pa didn't come to know the Lord until he was an adult, whereas Ma was raised in the faith. When Pa's eye first fell on Ma — and hers on him — she couldn't have anything to do with him because he wasn't a Christian. When Ma asked her father if Pa could go to church with her, he said, "No. If he really wants to go to church, he better go alone. Then we can see if he's just going for you." Pa emigrated to Canada, then was called back to the Netherlands during World War I, and finally Ma's father relented a bit. He began to see that Pa was searching sincerely. He helped Pa learn what Christianity is all about, and eventually he blessed the couple's marriage.

So Pa, unlike Ma, became a Christian without all the baggage that second- and third-generation Calvinists bring with them when they confess Christ as their Savior. This difference was obvious in the do's and don'ts in our family. Pa's ideas were based on principles and interpretations that he had worked out. Ma's ideas were solidly based on principles and interpretations, too, but hers were interlaced with the customs and traditions of strong Dutch Calvinists. However different their ideas were, Ma prevailed. Her ideas ruled the family.

On Tuesdays and Thursdays Pa finished his route by noon or one o'clock. On Thursday afternoons he worked in the yard or did the little things Ma couldn't do (repairing screens, washing the high windows, doing minor remodeling jobs, and so on); sometimes in the summer he took us on family outings in the truck. When he was in a very good mood, he would even remove all the racks and drawers from the inside of the truck and let us take a couple of friends along.

Although Pa tried hard to please Ma in every way, on one thing he was adamant: Tuesday afternoons were his. On those afternoons — whether it was rainy or sunny, snowy or windy, below freezing or steamy — Pa went fishing with his buddies. Usually Ma agreed that Pa needed this time to himself, but sometimes she resented it.

On these fishing trips, the men discussed, argued over, and settled all the church's problems. Pa had gotten only a fourth-grade education in the Netherlands, but he loved ideas, and he learned to read English very well, so he kept up with current issues, both religious and political. He read the daily newspaper, the weekly church magazine, a political news magazine (Democratic), and religious books. He and his friends argued as much as they fished — about Christianity, Calvinism, Christian education, politics, and more. *"Ja,"* Pa joked, "if they would only listen to us. . . ." During the Depression years, the fishing buddies argued long and loudly about the Townsend Plan, the bankers who robbed the common people, the Social Security act, and which political party had caused the Depression. (Pa was an avid Democrat until later years, when poverty no longer stalked him.) No matter how much these men argued, they always went fishing again.

Pa was a good thinker, and he shared his thoughts generously — too generously, Ma thought. She worried about what people would think of him. He was often on the Christian school board, and he devoted himself to it, especially during the Depression years. But during that time he was never elected an elder in the church. He didn't mind that much; the Christian school was his first love. But Ma minded, and she blamed Pa as well as the church; she told him that if he wanted to be elected, he had to keep his mouth shut. Part of her was humiliated that he wasn't elected, and another part of her was disappointed, because she knew what a good elder he would be. Later on, though, when we children were much older and the Christian school didn't take all Pa's energies and vocal defenses, he did become an elder. He served well for many years.

I loved Pa very much, but he disappointed me twice. My first disappointment involved advice that he gave my older brother, Bernie. Pa took his commitment to Christ seriously, and every now and then we talked together about serving the Lord. Still, after Bernie had earned his doctorate in chemistry, and he consulted Pa about two employment opportunities, it seemed to me that Pa had forgotten what he had taught me. Should he accept an offer he had to teach in a Christian college, Bernie asked Pa, or accept a position in a large corporation? For financial reasons, Pa said, the corporate position would be best. And that's what Bernie chose. It turned out to be excellent advice, but at the time I was disillusioned. What had happened to Pa's priorities? I wondered sadly. My second disappointment came when he refused to allow me to prepare for college.

My illness hurt Pa deeply, but he remained very supportive of me. Later on, between the times I was hospitalized, he would often drop by alone, and we would have a cup of tea. I was comfortable with him. I loved him, and I *felt* his love for me.

It wasn't hard to talk with my doctor about Pa. I wondered whether I had inherited any of *his* goodness. Usually people said, "You're just like your mother." Ray had said so, and even Pa had made that remark on more than one occasion. I hated being told that; nothing hurt me more.

Even as I finished telling my doctor about Pa, my thoughts

raced ahead to Ma. Would I be able to talk about her? What would I say?

I returned to my room, again with my stomach churning and my head pounding. Although this session with the doctor had been one of the easier ones, I was sick at heart. The fifth commandment, "Honor your father and your mother," blazed across my brain. I shook violently.

I had to see my pastor.

A Flicker of Courage

O send your Spirit now, dear Lord, to me,
that he may touch my eyes and make me see.
Show me the truth made plain within your Word,
for in your book revealed I see you, Lord.

"Break Now the Bread
of Life," stanza 4

IT WAS A COUPLE OF DAYS before my minister could come to see me. I felt like there was a hole inside me that clutched me in its bottomless depths. Three months had passed since my first day in the hospital. As far as I could see, I was no better, perhaps worse. Life was starless and moonless. I couldn't find the light switch, and God didn't turn it on for me. I yearned for what never could be, and my body ached with loneliness. Would I ever understand why I exist? Like a dog that endlessly chases a tail he cannot reach, my thoughts pursued the peace I never would know. I knew I had to continue, but I felt stuck on the path my doctor was leading me down. I couldn't go back; I couldn't go forward. I was mired in the Slough of Despond.

I feared people. The few visitors who now came to see me came with my doctor's permission. Actually I dreaded any visitor except my husband. I clutched him with a desperation that wounded him each time he came. He never tried to correct my distorted thinking; he only comforted me and listened to my whining again and again.

I was plagued by self-doubt. Some days my body couldn't contain its agony. It seemed to separate itself from me, from life itself. "I" gazed at "me," and observed how she writhed. It was like watching myself on television. I needed help, but I didn't want anyone to stop my body's flight from itself. In a perverse sort of way, the separation quieted me.

Still, my earlier yearning for death and oblivion didn't return. I was moving, however weakly, toward mental health.

Meanwhile, thinking about exploring my relationship with Ma was creating havoc. I couldn't do it. It would be too wicked to talk about her. Even if she never found out about it, God would never forgive me. Besides, to talk about her, I would probably have to talk about myself, and I dreaded that even more. Thoroughly mixed up with my thoughts about my mother was the fear that I would never get my children back.

Today whole families are involved in therapy when one member is ill. "Dysfunctional families," they are called. Some are profoundly dysfunctional, some only mildly so. There are some researchers who estimate that as many as 80 percent of America's families are "dysfunctional" to some degree. But there wasn't such a thing as family therapy when I was in the hospital; besides, the members of the family of my childhood were all adults now with children of their own. In my case, it was I who was ill, not my family. It wasn't their fault; it was mine. Maybe Case No. 5352 was a statistic somewhere, but I knew it was the mentally unbalanced me.

The prospect of exploring my subconscious frightened me, because I knew it held the truth about me. But I knew I had to do it. According to David Viscott, author of *The Makings of a Psychiatrist,* "Nothing hurts more than a wound that cuts through the illusion and makes you see through yourself." This was the pain I had to face. Talking about me would make no sense unless I talked about my mother first. I knew what my next step would have to be.

I was glad when my minister finally came for another visit. He provided the space and safety I needed to get to the point. It didn't take long before we edged to the topic of mothers.

"Will I ever be a mother again to my children?" I asked him.

"Of course."

"But will I be a *good* mother?"

"Of course," he replied. "After this illness passes, you will be an even better mother than you were before — and you're a good mother now," he assured me.

He knew my mother, and he enjoyed her; in fact, he was a very good friend of both my parents. I mumbled about my problem with feeling disloyal if I talked about Ma, and my problem with the fifth commandment. I told him that I was beginning to feel angry with Ma — in however vague and unstructured a way — and I knew this was sinful. "Needing to honor my parents and feeling angry — they're really rolled up in one," I said.

In *The Roots of Sorrow,* Richard Winter observes that "many more women than men get seriously depressed. This may be partly due to the fact that most women tend to internalize their anger and frustration whereas many men find external outlets for their emotions. It is interesting that while there are more women than men admitted to psychiatric hospitals, there are many more men than women in prison." I learned much later that anger is most dangerous, destructive, and damaging to its owner . . . and that was me! Its damage multiplies when an individual internalizes it and doesn't have an opportunity to work it out. Its evil increases even more when its very *presence* is denied, consciously or subconsciously. Then it can become an emotional cancer that can destroy the whole person. It weakens and it ruins. It wreaks havoc with relationships. The diagnosis usually can't be made without professional help — I'm a prime example.

The minister agreed with me that it seemed like my anger and my need to honor my parents were mixed up together, but, he said, "It's not that big a problem that we can't disentangle it." He explained that anger itself is not necessarily sin. Not sin? I didn't believe him.

"The Bible speaks about anger and how to handle it," he went on. "Ephesians 4:26 says, 'In your anger do not sin.' The fact that you know you're angry is the important first step. You can't do much with anger you don't know you have, can you?" he asked.

My minister also pointed out that "honoring" parents doesn't mean that children have to deny that their parents are human and have flaws, make mistakes, and yes, even sin. I should know that much about parents, I thought. I felt a flicker of hope. Strange that such sensible — and biblical — thoughts lay so deeply buried within me.

"There's a great difference between honoring your parents as a child and doing so as an adult," my minister continued. "Part of honoring your parents lies in being or becoming an independent, healthy, Christian adult. It would be less than honorable to harbor secret thoughts and feelings and anger if it prevented you from becoming a whole person again. The writer of Ephesians also said, 'Do not let the sun go down while you are still angry.' I suggest that you not only may but that you must talk with the doctor about your mother."

My minister didn't pry. He simply encouraged me to tell the doctor about all my memories and feelings as they surfaced. "It may well be," he said, "that your mother made mistakes when you were growing up. I know she would want to correct them if she could."

I recoiled in horror at this; there was no way I would ever discuss with her the memories that were now agitating me. My face burned.

My pastor's visit was almost over; the time had gone quickly. He prayed for me, asking God to give me the courage to say what would be helpful to recovery and to give me the peace to know that he would bless this courage. I understood his prayer (an accomplishment by itself), but I didn't feel serene afterward. And yet, I didn't explode in rage. I couldn't even say, "Yes, I'm very angry." As he was leaving, I thought to myself, maybe I'll get my courage up before my next therapy session.

But after he had gone, I lost what little control I still had. I started thinking that I was crazy and would be hospitalized for life. A nurse saw how upset I was and gave me a sedative.

What would I say? What could I say? How could I talk about *her?*

Ma

She watches over the affairs of her household
and does not eat the bread of idleness. . . .
A woman who fears the Lord is to be praised.

Proverbs 31:27, 30

MA WAS A GOOD WOMAN. Although she was often sick and suffered broken bones more than a dozen times, she was strong physically. She was also strong in her convictions, her loyalties, her devotion to duty, and her discipline. She taught her children thoroughly. The two lessons I learned best from Ma were the importance of work and the importance of obedience.

Ma usually looked intense. She had piercing, gray-green eyes, and her lips, usually compressed, disappeared when she was angry. I'm sure her hair wasn't always gray, or the beautiful white it turned when she was older, but that's how I remember it. She was tall for a woman (about five feet, eight or nine inches), and solidly built, but she carried her weight well. When I was a child, I thought she was regal and powerful.

Although she was a practical woman, she stayed abreast of fads and fancies, and when she began wearing lipstick — just a little — her lips formed a thin horizontal rectangle, precisely bisected.

Ma loved to look stylish, and she preferred to buy fewer and better clothes. Pa encouraged her to think of herself, and not of money; he never begrudged her spending money on herself, and she never abused his encouragement. He enjoyed the pleasure she took in her appearance. But no matter how hard he tried to make her happy, he didn't often see Ma truly enjoying life. Ma saw her cup as half empty; she always needed more.

She didn't allow herself or her home to be untidy. Every day except Sunday she spent the early morning hours picking up or cleaning the house. She believed that a woman's "dirty work" — her expression for housecleaning — should be done by ten o'clock, which was coffee time. That's when she took off her dustcap, removed her curlers, and arranged her pompadour for the day. The only exceptions were the days she did her spring cleaning.

Ma was a good cook, although supper was a pretty predictable meal at our house. On Tuesday nights when Pa went fishing, she would cook some of the things we children liked: baked beans and corn muffins, or meat loaf and scalloped potatoes. But otherwise she didn't vary the menu because Pa wanted just meat, potatoes, vegetables, and yellow pudding. Ma browned the meat to perfection, and Pa insisted that the meat drippings be left as they were, not thickened into gravy. As for the potatoes, they had to be boiled — not baked, mashed, or fried, but boiled. Pa preferred Idahoes; it was his one insistence on luxury. Except for the roughest years of the Depression, Idahoes were a must. Sometimes, if the potatoes weren't to his liking, he would ask, "Not Idahoes, are they?" Then Ma would realize she had skimped too much.

She was an artist with crafts. Knitting was part of her life, and she also embroidered, crocheted, and tatted. She contributed woolen mittens, scarves, and hats by the bushel to various charities. Hundreds of babies wore booties and sweaters she made and donated. She needed no patterns; if she saw a garment, she could copy it.

Ma could do much with little. Efficient, frugal housekeeping was part of her religion. She kept the house tidy and the family neatly dressed, even during the Depression years. Often, without the benefit of patterns to help her, she "refashioned" old clothes that Pa brought home from his customers. As any seamstress or tailor knows, it's much more difficult to "make over" clothes than it is to sew from new fabrics and patterns. The finished garments were often ugly and ill-fitting, and I hated them — but Ma did her best.

Ma was a budget manager unequaled, although her thrift didn't always produce the most attractive results. One time she had the living and dining room carpets dyed. They were threadbare, and a door-to-door salesman had persuaded her that if he dyed them, they would look like new. But after he dyed them green, they looked as worn as ever — only now they were the color of bile. The salesman left a bucket of dye behind, and Ma, undeterred by the color, dipped several pairs of mittens, a couple of scarves, and even a sweater into the bucket. We three oldest children, who had to wear these "transformed" items, were reminded daily of her thrift.

Ma was serious, but she also knew how to enjoy herself. She didn't laugh often; even her smiles were scarce. But when she did laugh, her whole body laughed with her. And so did we. Sometimes we teased her about the telltale "Dutchness" of her pronunciation of English — she would put a "c" where an "h" belonged in some words (*scrimp, scrubbery, scutters*) — and she accepted our ribbing good-naturedly. She loved to play games. "Cards" were from the devil, but when canasta became the rage, she played with zest. *"Ja,"* she would say, "but this is different. You don't gamble with canasta." She liked playing Rook and dominoes, too; she loved to win and often did. She also enjoyed going fishing with Pa, and no one could fry fresh fish the way she could.

Because Ma always championed honoring one's parents, I often wondered why, in 1913, her filial obligations had not prevented her, then a single eighteen-year-old woman, from leaving her father's hearth in the Netherlands to follow her heart. Her love — my father — had emigrated to Canada. To be near him, Ma moved to Edmonton and lived with her brother and his family; she made some money by doing housework for others. When World War I broke out, all young Dutchmen, including her sweetheart, had to return to the Netherlands to serve in the army there, and Ma became very lonely. So she returned to the Netherlands, traveling aboard a ship with some 1200 soldiers — against the advice of her minister and the elders. She married her love in 1920 — after he became a Christian. And shortly after their first child was born, Ma and Pa emigrated to America, the land of opportunity.

Ma cared deeply for the family in the Netherlands (Pa and Ma were the only ones in their families, besides Ma's brother, who emigrated), and she missed them. She wrote faithfully to her brothers and sisters (and Pa's), even when they didn't. After World War II, she sent dozens and dozens of food packages to their thirteen brothers and sisters in the Netherlands, demonstrating her concern.

In her new country, the old, established ways of family and church became her fortress, her protection. Her brand of Christianity — Reformed Calvinism — and the customs, patterns, and traditions of the old country were the bricks of the enclave she erected for her family. The bricks were indiscriminately mortared together so that it was impossible for her to separate the bricks of belief from those of custom and tradition. If the church had permitted "watch-women" in those days, Ma would have been a sentry on the walls of Zion. No thief in the night could have slithered past her keen eye.

Ma knew that within these walls lay THE way of truth and righteousness. Her surveillance served a dual purpose. Not only would the pagans be barred from her fortress, but also none of her family would depart from Zion, not while she was in charge. No child of hers would climb over the wall or break it down, not even a little. She knew that God wanted it that way, and she would help him. Ma was strong.

Ma's misunderstanding of Calvinism undergirded her deep convictions. Her misunderstanding is perfectly described by Dr. I. John Hesselink in *On Being Reformed: Distinctive Characteristics and Common Misunderstandings*:

> In many Dutch American Reformed churches . . . sabbatarianism and other forms of legalism have certainly been all too characteristic of faith and piety. A good Christian was one who went to church twice on Sunday, did not do anything else on "the Sabbath" except take naps and read Christian literature, and one who during the week stayed away from worldly amusements such as the tavern, theater, and dance hall. . . . A further characteristic was great emphasis on purity of doctrine with little corresponding emphasis on the fruit of the Spirit and the joy of the Lord.

Ma had been raised in a humble, strict, Calvinist home in the Netherlands, and she feared the wickedness in America. Any deviation from her ideas of right and wrong had to be nipped in the bud, and she took her pruning seriously, in and out of season. Any infraction of her rules had dire consequences

— and those rules extended to what was and wasn't proper for females. She warned us continually of our eternal accountability: "You must answer for yourself." My debt grew daily.

Once I became a mother, I was sure that Ma often said too much and later regretted her words. She left nothing for the Lord to say. I came to this realization because I've done the same thing far too often.

Frequently Ma and Pa didn't see eye to eye on discipline. Ma knew instantly what was right; Pa needed time to consider the situation at hand. But he always supported Ma when she disciplined us in his absence. Ma demanded obedience — prompt and total. She expected us to *listen,* not talk. Any effort to explain was impertinent backtalk. (In her *Clinical Handbook of Depression,* Janice Wood Wetzel points out that if one person tries to make another respond passively and not express his or her true feelings, those feelings "will appear in a disguised form that is destructive to the self as well as to others." Depression is one of those "disguised forms.")

Ma found it especially hard to forgive us children. She took our disobedience very personally, and she frequently reminded us that we had hurt her long after the offending incident. In a corner of the kitchen she kept a stick visible and handy. She firmly believed that "those who spare the rod hate their children, but those who love them are diligent to discipline them" (Prov. 13:24, NRSV).

Ma was not only concerned about God's instructions for raising children. She seemed equally anxious about what other people would think of us. What would people think if we kids didn't sit still in church? If we didn't get good grades in school? If we behaved badly? If she had to shout too loudly to get us in for supper? If our clothes weren't clean and well mended? If I acted like a boy all the time?

Ma's anger at me was often triggered by my tomboyish

74

behavior. She knew the role I would have to fill as an adult female, and her sense of responsibility made clear her obligation to God, to me, and to herself. Her determination was second to none: her daughter *would* be a good Christian mother and wife. (How sadly funny it was that I was now in a hospital, all mixed up about what I as a mother and a Christian should be.)

Sometimes I thought Ma, like God, could see everything. As a child I didn't like this attribute of God, and I didn't like it in Ma, either. It made me afraid. To me it was the same eye. I had little privacy, little room to do anything Ma didn't first approve.

Sometimes my parents had spats. With Pa too, Ma found it hard to forgive; it took two, three, sometimes even four days for family life to return to normal. She finally would forgive Pa, but she would never verbalize it. She would never say, "I'm sorry." She'd get a little quieter, and she might make a special red currant sauce for Pa's favorite pudding.

Ma loved Pa and us kids, but her love had hard edges. There was little kissing and hugging in our family. Pa kissed Ma hello and good-bye and called her by endearing names, but Ma, although she accepted Pa's affection, rarely returned it. She did give her all to her family, although she seldom showed that she enjoyed it. Working for the family was her living sacrifice. "Everything I do, I'm doing for you," she often said.

Ma was always concerned about the health of her children, but no one got away with faking sickness. If one of us didn't feel like going to school or wanted to get out of some unpleasant work, we knew better than to pretend we didn't feel good — she always knew. The cure was worse than the reason for faking.

But when we were really sick, she was kind and gentle. She kept the bedding fresh. She held our heads when we were racked by nausea. She brought us cold juice or warm tea. She even gave us rusks, which were a treat. And when it was "the wrong time of the month" for me, she was gentle and sympathetic. It was something only women could understand, Ma said.

Why, I asked my doctor, couldn't I say I loved my mother? So much about her was good! Why then did it hurt so much to talk about her, even think about her? Why did I feel so hesitant — and compelled — to tell him about her flaws? He said nothing, and I surely didn't know.

My recollections on these pages seem calm, but my actual recounting was filled with tears and emotional explosions. I wanted so much to be fair to Ma. My doctor commented that we were making progress, but that we had done enough for one session — we had been talking for more than two hours. I had become agitated and wanted to keep talking, but he suggested that we continue "next time."

I reached my room before I retched and became sick. A sedative calmed me. Much later I began to think of next time. I knew I had to say more about Ma.

Biblically speaking, Ma was not the head of our family, of course, but practically speaking, she was. Describing Sundays and Mondays in our house, which were night-and-day different, would demonstrate how the family revolved around Ma.

I would tell my doctor about them next time.

Sunday and Monday

What causes fights and quarrels among you?

James 4:1

THE DAYS I SPENT in school being taught by Christian instructors played an important role in shaping the kind of adult I would become. But the days that most shaped my mental outlook and emotional tendencies were Sundays and Mondays.

"Remember the Sabbath day, to keep it holy." That command to holiness involved specific do's and don'ts, and Ma knew which ones were holy.

The Sabbath was a bittersweet day, because Ma equated the Commandments with the do's and don'ts of Dutch Calvinist traditions and legalisms. Once I asked her about the meaning of the verse which says that "the Sabbath was made for man." Ma thought that was impertinence, not natural childish curiosity, and she answered my question with a slap.

The longest *do*, of course, was church twice every Sunday. Just *going* to church with Ma was difficult. It was hard for a girl to put her hat on straight and keep it that way, to walk without pointing her toes in, to keep her lower lip pulled in, to hold her purse still, to keep her gloves clean, to turn hymn pages without making noise — the list seemed endless. Ma asked me why she had to remind me about these things Sunday after Sunday, and I didn't have an answer. I didn't know.

Ma was very concerned about how her husband and five children looked as we marched in precise order into "our pew" every Sunday. I had to sit next to Ma, because girls sit by their mothers. I wanted to sit next to Pa or at the end of the pew, but that wasn't proper. Since I sat next to Ma, she could observe all of my moving around, my yawns, my twitchings. She would look at me sternly to try to get me to stop, and if that wasn't enough, she would pinch me.

The church service put a lot of questions in my head — silly ones, I guess. I wondered why the minister wore a long black coat with a slit up the back. And why he never folded his hands for prayer. And why, when he led the congregational prayer, he leaned back, rested one hand on his oak throne, and kept his left hand in his pocket while he rambled on. I didn't think of asking Ma about that because then she would know I had opened my eyes during prayer — another don't.

For children, there is no other place on earth where time passes as slowly as it does in church. I couldn't understand why the clock had to be in the back of the church. The minister never looked at it; if he had, I was sure he would have timed his sermons better. Every so often, when it seemed like a couple of hours or more must have gone by, I tried to turn my head subtly to check on the time. Of course, Ma poked me each time, but what was worse, the hands of the clock had inched ahead only a minute or two. Three peppermints, even when I rationed them, were hardly enough for the one-and-a-half to two hours the service lasted. There were no children's bulletins then, and I wasn't allowed to have a pencil or paper to make notes. Children were to be seen in church, but they couldn't be active, and they certainly weren't supposed to be heard.

I did love the music of the pipe organ. Sometimes I wished the minister would pipe down so the organ could pipe up for a bigger part of the service. I enjoyed singing from *The Psalter,* our church's official songbook for worship services. In 1934 or 1935 our church bought copies of the new *Psalter Hymnal,* and I was excited by the change, because for the first time the songbook contained hymns in addition to the Psalms.

But the music didn't make up for the sermons. Once each Sunday the minister based his sermon on the Heidelberg Catechism, which is one of the doctrinal standards of the church to which I belonged. As I heard them, the sermons supported Ma's "thou shalt nots." Not until after my illness did I see the beautiful side of this catechism. Whether the preacher emphasized only the gloomy side or whether my child's ear absorbed only the thunder and doom, I don't know. In any case, what I absorbed molded my adolescent concept of God as a demanding, vengeful being who punished all of our sins, either now or later or now *and* later. Usually the minister chose a single verse as the basis for his sermon, which didn't give him much range in his topic. Very often the text he chose threatened and disturbed rather than inspired or comforted — and I took the threats personally.

I learned that nothing is good unless it is *all* for God. If something isn't totally good, it's totally bad. People, events, and things are either all white or all black (this, of course, was before I learned how negative my use of the word *black* was). God's eyes saw no gray. Little did I know then that this idea was a weed that would one day choke my spiritual garden.

As I grew older, I had many questions — some serious, some not so serious — about both Christianity and the church.

Why, I wondered, did God even think of letting Abraham kill Isaac? How did Noah get all those animals in the ark? Was it fair to have Samson kill all those Philistines? How come David could still be a king even after he killed Uriah, but our church said that if a person got divorced, he or she couldn't belong to our church? Why did God send his son to die on the cross instead of going himself? When someone slaps your cheek, why should you turn the other one? If the treasures we lay up in heaven aren't made of gold, where will the gold for the streets of heaven come from? These and many more questions crowded my mind. But Ma often considered my questions impertinent, even fresh. It was easier to get answers from my teachers in school.

Gradually I realized how badly I sinned every day, even while I was in church, supposedly worshipping God. I could never be the kind of Christian that the minister preached about; I gave God too much pain. I wouldn't be able to meet God's expectations any more than I could meet Ma's. I didn't know whose expectations I cared more about, but what did it matter? I didn't please either one. Was it even worth trying? Then I would recall something my mother said to me frequently — "Remember, *meid,* you'll have to account for it some day" — and I would try again. Even when I was very young, this reminder was very troubling to me. God is perfect, I learned, and his children had to be perfect too. I worried a lot.

Still, Sunday was special because it was the only day we had *dinner.* Every other day of the week we had *supper* at our house. Ma insisted it was supper, even when I explained what *dinner* meant. I wanted to call it *dinner* because that sounded more American, but Ma said I was putting on airs.

But Sunday dinner at our house was an occasion a young American could be proud of — and I was. Over the years Ma had acquired everything needed to set a lovely table: a beautiful, light-blue tablecloth with matching napkins, Noritake china, 1847 Rogers silverware, and Fostoria crystal goblets. The menu too was special. Ma would cook the roast to perfection, and sometimes she even saved a little of the drippings for Pa and thickened the rest into gravy. (Before serving the roast, Ma always cut a thick slice for Pa's Monday supper, because only Pa had meat on Monday.) Besides potatoes (Idahoes, of course), Ma served two vegetables. Often these were green beans, on which she dabbed "real butter" (not margarine) and a little nutmeg, and cauliflower, which she covered with white sauce and sprinkled with paprika. A molded jello salad (very fancy in those days), dinner rolls (we had bread during the week), and relishes completed the meal. And, of course, Ma made dessert, often trying something new.

Sunday dinner was a treat I never tired of, and I loved having guests on that day. Often we entertained schoolteachers, friends of the family, and friends of us kids. We joked and laughed, and occasionally the adults discussed serious issues of the church or the Christian school. It was always a pleasant experience.

But after dinner, the rest of Sunday moved slowly. The don'ts prevailed. Don't get dirty. Don't play rough. Don't walk up the avenue. (The avenue near our church and school was lined with retail stores. Even though the shades were drawn on Sunday — since most of the stores were owned by Dutch Calvinists — the stores represented something forbidden on the Sabbath.) Don't. Do. Don't. Do. Going to church at night was a *Do*. If we kids wanted to "skip," we had to come up with defensible, creative reasons for doing it — and we were rarely successful.

All told, Sunday was primarily negative — not, I hoped, a "foretaste of glory divine." Yet so ingrained in my mind was the need for specified, inflexible Sunday conduct that I insisted on these same rigid legalisms for many years while Ray and I were raising our children. But that changed one Sunday afternoon in 1960. We had moved to Phoenix a few months earlier. We had bought a house with a large swimming pool — but of course we didn't swim on Sunday. But this was an afternoon in July, and the thermometer registered 115 degrees. "I'm going in the pool," Ray announced, "no matter what you say." The children, of course, were delighted.

Surprisingly, after talking about this, I didn't feel bad. It was another burst of growth in the seed planted by the doctor. I felt released, enlightened. I was beginning to experience the loosening of the legalism that had constrained much of my life and had robbed me of knowing the Father who wanted his children to enjoy him.

*   *   *

If Sundays were negative at our house, then Mondays were awful — whether it was winter or summer, whether we kids had school or summer vacation. Maybe school days were a little better because at least then I could leave the house and be gone for most of the day.

Maybe Ma didn't discipline us kids excessively on Mondays — I don't know. But as I recall, most of the slaps, spankings for minor wrongs, and whippings happened on Monday.

What made Mondays so bad was Ma's single-minded determination to get all of the family laundry done. She felt that by Monday night she had to do all the washing and ironing, finish all the mending and darning, and put all the clean clothes away! Trying to accomplish this took every ounce of her energy and every minute of her time. When she didn't succeed — and often she didn't — it upset her and the whole week.

The weekly laundry was huge. Ma kept her family's clothes clean and pressed, which was no small task with five kids and no clothes that were permanent-press. When I was ten, she taught me how to iron; from then on it became my task to help her each Monday. When she got a mangle (a machine for ironing laundry by passing it between heated rollers), she taught me how to use that. During summer vacation I could give her more help, and that made her workday shorter.

Two things drove Ma crazy on Monday: one was bad weather. When I got out of bed on Monday morning, the first thing I did was check the weather. If it was raining or snowing, I shivered. Bad weather — and Michigan's weather was bad frequently — got in Ma's way and made her cranky. Rain meant that she couldn't hang the laundry outdoors and it wouldn't dry soon enough for her to iron that same day. Snow presented a different problem. Ma could hang the clothes outside, but she couldn't count on their staying clean. There were train yards at one end of our street and a refrigerator factory at the other — and both produced soot that would settle on the laundry. When the soot combined with the snow, the clothes would get dirty, and Ma would often have to re-rinse them.

When Monday's schedule went awry, then Tuesday's did too, and the domino effect didn't disappear until late Wednesday. Sometimes she had to give up a Wednesday morning coffee date, something she enjoyed and hated to surrender. (Kaffeeklatsching was her recreation, though she didn't spend much time doing it. After I married, one of Ma's big disappointments was that I didn't have coffee with her frequently enough. "My only daughter," she often said, "and what do I have with her? Nothing.")

The other thing that drove Ma to distraction on Monday was her fighting children. Ma grudgingly accepted that God controlled the weather, but it was her job to control the children — which was quite a task, since we were bad more often than the weather. On Monday, God's job was easier. Ma wasn't too

83

successful with us, except when she used her ever-handy stick, which she did often.

We children seemed to fight more on Monday mornings, and we did so without mercy and without consideration for Ma. It wasn't a nice way to start the week. We helped ourselves to breakfast — usually from a pan of oatmeal Ma had made. Breakfast was not without quibbling: *You're taking too much sugar. Hey, you're not supposed to use the butter — that's for Pa. Give me back my knife. Get your elbows out of my territory. It's your turn to put the food away. Quit touching my leg. I'm going to tell, and then you'll get it. Stop looking at me like that.* Then followed the usual pandemonium of who was first in the bathroom, who was taking too long, who wasn't brushing his teeth, who was calling someone else a name. With Pa already gone on his route and Ma working in the basement, it seemed like a perfect time to quarrel. When we did this, we were asking for trouble. Ma hated to be interrupted when she was doing laundry. Sometimes she would holler at us from the basement; sometimes we would hear her heavy tread on the stairs and know what we were in for. My brothers don't remember these occasions very well — but I do. Maybe I was punished more than they were. And maybe I deserved it — I don't know. But I have painful memories of these times.

Often I went to school tense or crying because I had started the week displeasing Ma. If I had been particularly bad in the morning, I hurried home as fast as I could after school. Ma's mood of the morning usually hadn't changed, and she'd put me to work right away.

I recall a Monday when I was in second grade. I had dawdled over breakfast and put off getting dressed for school, so that I didn't have time to clear the table. The boys had already left, and Ma came upstairs to see what I was doing. She saw the uncleared table and then noticed I wasn't ready for school. Furious, she took the stick from the kitchen corner and whipped my legs. I was so distracted by my crying that I put my dress on inside out and went to school that way. When some of the other children laughed at me, I started to cry — again. My teacher took me to the cloakroom, helped me with my dress, and excused me so that I could dab my eyes and get a drink.

I always prayed for Tuesday to come quickly, but it never did. How many of my prayers had been for nothing, I wondered. Even my mealtime "GodblessthisfoodforJesussakeamen" might have been worthless. I wondered if God played tricks on people whose prayers were just words. Maybe I wasn't able to be good because my prayers were worthless. Maybe I wasn't pleasing God, and that's why I couldn't please Ma. I thought a lot about prayer when I was a child. I just didn't know much about God. I had no hope that he would answer the prayers of a naughty girl.

Ma didn't say much of anything appreciative to us kids on Mondays, and it never occurred to us to express appreciation for what she was trying to accomplish. We each had our Monday chores, so maybe we felt we were doing our part. I found little ways to rebel against the rigid routine: although I had to come home immediately after school every Monday to help Ma, I didn't always hurry. The one exception to the routine came when my eighth-grade teacher asked me to stay after school on Mondays to study with her. Because my parents had great respect for my teachers, they allowed this — but I remember how disappointed it made Ma.

Although it always exhausted Ma to try to finish all of the laundry on Monday, she never gave up this compulsion. But eventually my brothers and I grew up and left home, and the laundry did become easier for her to manage. With a lighter load, an automatic washer and dryer, and a mangle, her work was cut in half. Still, whenever holidays fell on Monday and threw her off schedule, she was a bit befuddled for several days.

Although my brothers remember Mondays with some chuckles, I remember Mondays with horror. To me Ma was a Monday-morning bear, handy with a stick, who could give us one or more painful whacks. I can't say for sure, but I think that as a little girl I cried more on Monday than on any other day.

As I thought about this and made notes to discuss with my doctor, I wondered: Just what was wrong with me, as a message receiver, that made Monday so traumatic for me and not for my brothers?

Although I didn't realize it then, my memories of Sunday and Monday were enfolding me in a cocoon so tight that someday my doctor would have to therapeutically remove that covering before I could emerge to become what God intended me to be.

Fear

On whom but God can we rely,
the One who sits enthroned on high,
who condescends to see and know
the things of heaven and earth below?

"Praise God, You Servants
of the Lord," stanza 3

APRIL HAD DISAPPEARED into May — and I wondered if I was moving forward or backward. After talking about Pa and Ma, I felt as though I had revealed my worst secrets to my doctor. I thought that my depression might lift — but I was wrong. I was consumed by sadness, anxiety, and fear. Attempting to recognize and acknowledge the anger deep within me was a huge struggle.

I had hoped that my new understanding would give me quick relief. But healing from depression is neither fast nor dramatic. When it didn't come, my fear kept growing.

I had made enough progress in my therapy to understand certain things about the time Ray and I had spent in Nigeria.

No longer did I think that missionaries are superior Christians, above the squabbles and petty disagreements that typically mar human relations. I understood that I was not the cause of everything that had gone awry there. I saw that my anger about what had happened was justified — although I hadn't handled it well. I also saw that both my illness and my failings had contributed to my inability to accept the tension and frustration that comes with the closeness of compound living.

Maybe I *understood* this situation better now, but understanding is not forgiving — and I still couldn't forgive the people in Nigeria who had hurt me. Forgiving is not merely an act of mind and mouth. It requires time and conviction.

I finally realized that the sources of my illness went much deeper than my Nigerian experience. But it seemed to me that I had made little if any progress in uncovering those deeper sources. At this point I didn't see that talking about my mother had accomplished much.

And I still felt alienated from God. I now believed that I could call myself a Christian. But I didn't feel the comfort of God's love. God still loomed as Judge, not as Father. The psalmist articulated how I felt:

> I remembered you, O God, and I groaned;
> I mused, and my spirit grew faint.
> You kept my eyes from closing;
> I was too troubled to speak. . . .
> Will [you] never show [your] favor again? . . .
> [Have you] forgotten to be merciful?
> [Have you] in anger withheld [your] compassion?
> (Ps. 77:3-4, 7, 9)

I pondered my rage, even though I hated to acknowledge its presence. It wasn't Christian to lose one's temper, I knew, and I rarely lost mine. That hadn't always been the case. I had learned to control my temper, not because I was such a good Christian but because I paid a heavy physical price for losing my temper. I suffered from migraine headaches even in the best of times (and it would take me one or two days to recover from one), and an explosion of temper could easily bring on a migraine. I thought that squelching my anger was a good way to handle it; I didn't know how wrong I was. Later on, when I read *The Christian's Handbook of Psychiatry* by O. Quentin Hyder, I came across a passage in which he explains what I was experiencing:

> The ambivalence resulting from both love and rage, with accompanying feelings of guilt, cannot be expressed or even admitted consciously, and that leads to hostility and anger turned inward. This self-punishment results in depression. . . . It is also a cry for help. . . . The patient's real self cannot handle the angry feelings adequately.

One day, I found myself standing in the hall, tired in every way I could think of. I was losing whatever control I had been gaining, and it took all of my energy to appear calm. Even in the hospital I didn't want others to see my inability to control myself. Little did I realize then that I, like my mother, worried about what other people would say. Nor did I realize how much this tendency to bottle up my feelings for appearance's sake had sapped my vigor and spontaneity in Nigeria.

I went back to my room, fell on my bed, and started to cry. Once I started crying, I couldn't stop. My roommate summoned the nurse, who gave me a sedative.

At the time I was hospitalized, group sessions were not formally part of the therapy that patients received. But when I did feel like talking to someone besides the doctor, informal conversations with fellow patients provided some help and comfort. In the hospital there weren't the usual divisions you see in society. We didn't know who was educated or uneducated, smart or not so smart, rich or poor. Here everyone started at square one. We were all here because something had gone awry in our lives and we were too ill to live in the real world. Because of this common bond, we became friends, and we shared some of our problems and some of what our doctors had told us — although none of us shared our secrets with each other as fully as we did with our doctors. Sometimes we dried each other's tears, and frequently we shared hugs; an arm around the shoulder could sometimes stop the trembling. One time my father and my brother Gerry, who was a baker, brought enough cream puffs for all the patients and the nurses — especially the nurses.

The nurses were God's angels. They were always ready to comfort, to listen, and to call my doctor when I needed him. I appreciated the things they made bearable for me, and I grew to love them very much. One of the things that most impressed me about them was that they never hurried me. I had been in a hurry all of my life, working fast and without letup. As a child I had learned that hard work — like cleanliness — was next to godliness. But the nurses were never too busy with their work to make time for me. They were flexible when they could be. Of course, they couldn't unlock the front door when I asked them to, but they did help me overcome my anger at having to be confined in a mental hospital. Still, they couldn't help me handle the rage about other things growing inside me.

It was May, yes, but the rebirth of spring didn't bring me relief. I was still in the hospital. When would I overcome my fear? When would I feel hopeful again? Hopelessness is the worst and most stubborn element of depression. The few visitors I was allowed to have tried to cheer me. They talked about the beauties of the season and how happy I must be that spring had arrived — soon I would be able to walk outside. They didn't realize that if I got "outside," I wanted to be completely better and away from this place, not walking around its grounds under the guard of a nurse.

At this point in my illness, I still felt more comfortable in the hospital than outside it. I knew now that I was truly ill. Yet I also thought I was behaving badly, and I blamed myself for that. I had made my bed, and uncomfortable as it was, I had to lie in it.

Finally I began to recognize that the fear and rage which were growing inside me were related somehow to my feelings about my mother. At my next therapy session, my doctor and I discussed this. He made these notes about our conversation:

> Although she has a tendency to revert to these ideas [that I was the cause of my illness], she is beginning to see more and more that this condition which she is in is one of illness, although it is still difficult for her to accept it at times. She has a good deal of difficulty when she is out of the hospital with fears that someone will come to the door to whom she will have to talk or with whom she will have to visit, and she correctly states that she cannot be out of the hospital for any length of time, as she has to live in fear that the doorbell [or the telephone] will ring. She wants very much now to see this is an illness and at times does accept it and at such times she is markedly improved. This idea, however, is not as yet a part of her thinking in any deeply rooted way, with the obvious result that she fears being out in a group or even in small groups because of the self blame which she lays upon herself.
>
> This patient is constantly looking for a definite reason why she became ill, why this is so and why that is so, and

often expresses the idea that she must know the exact reasons that lie at the bottom of her illness, otherwise she cannot be satisfied and is convinced that she then will have a recurrence even if she should become superficially somewhat better.

It is obvious that she does not accept this emotional upheaval very well because of the intense fear which she shows even in the possibility of some unknown person coming to the door to whom she might have to speak and who might ask about her and her work or that of her husband on the mission field in Africa.

In general she is making some progress. I feel that [it will be some time] before this woman will be rehabilitated. I believe the prognosis, however, is fairly good. There is a meticulousness within her and also somewhat of a compulsion to have everything systematized and to know minute details before she can be satisfied, which are definite obstacles in the way of her recovery. On the other hand, she has an intense desire to be well. . . . She has a good memory and is highly intelligent. She tries to apply the things which are talked over with her. Sometimes these attempts are good and sometimes [they are] bad, depending on her approach or understanding. She proves to be a very interesting patient from a psychiatric standpoint, but also an exceedingly difficult one.

To her the hospital has become a place of refuge. She feels more at ease here than anywhere else. Sometimes going home for even a few hours on a visit causes intense fatigue. At other times she has no fatigue. In spite of this I believe that her recovery will be best served by continuing to allow her to have outside visits and overnight visits when possible.

My doctor told me that I had made progress, but I didn't see it. I had to admit, though, that when I looked back to the day when I woke up in the hospital and then looked at how I was now, I realized I had gained some insight into myself. With depression one cannot look back a week or a day and expect to see progress. One has to ask, "Am I better today than I was a month ago? three months ago? several months ago?"

During one session my doctor asked me about my relationship with Ray. I told him that it seemed to me that my happiness in life began when I met Ray. Although I was young — nineteen — when we were married, we had a very good marriage. On one occasion my doctor suggested to Ray that I had married young in order to get away from my mother; Ray was offended, and I have never agreed with that notion. I married Ray because I loved him: he is a man who is kind and gentle yet has a sense of adventure, a good husband who has always shown how much he cares about me, a good father, and a good provider. Talking about Ray made me think of how blessed I was to have him and our four children, and I berated myself for not being happy.

"Still not accepting this as illness, are you?" my doctor countered.

I looked at him and began to cry.

"Why am I always so scared?" I could understand that my illness could cause fear, but was fear itself the illness?

"Part of it, yes," the doctor replied. Then he suggested that I spend some more time examining my relationship with my mother.

"Must I?"

"No. There isn't anything you *must* do," he replied.

After that I left his office. It had been a long session. My appointment had begun at four, and an hour and a half had passed since my doctor had called his wife at five o'clock to tell her he didn't know when he would be home for dinner.

I felt grateful that he had spent this time with me . . . and guilty.

Like Mother, Like Daughter

Breathe on me, Breath of God,
until my heart is pure,
until with Thee I will Thy will,
to do and to endure.

"Breathe on Me, Breath of God,"
stanza 2

MY FEARS MULTIPLIED as my doctor and I moved nearer to exploring my relationship with Ma in greater depth. Even though I perceived the hospital as a refuge, I still somewhat resented being there and undergoing treatment. Besides, I thought, Christians should be able to talk to God in prayer and get answers. My minister had been praying for me, but God didn't answer.

I had never shared my pain with anyone except Ray. I often covered my feelings with too much talk. And from my teenage years on I had had frequent and severe migraines that would last for days at a time — why, I didn't know. Would my life ever change?

If I were really truthful, I had to admit that I wasn't eager to change myself. My mother had been trying to change me since the day I was born, and look what I was now. Any change I would make would only worsen my life, I reasoned. "Why shouldn't I be me?" I asked my doctor. "Because my mother doesn't like me the way I am?" I was confused.

On the other hand, I knew that if I didn't cooperate, I wouldn't get well. Perhaps the potential for change did lie within me. I had to dig deep to see. My relationship with my mother gnawed at me like a frenzied animal gnawing at his paw to escape a trap. Yet it seemed farfetched to me that Ma might be involved in my illness. Still, my doctor was right. Something within me had to be cut out. "Surgery," he said, "is painful, but often necessary if healing is to happen."

On some level I knew that he had identified the core problem; I just couldn't admit it. I respected my older brother, Bernie, very much and shared this burden with him. Bernie encouraged me to be honest and open about Ma. I said I would try, and I asked him to call my doctor and tell him a little bit about Ma. In response to Bernie's call, my doctor set up another session with me. In his file he made these comments about our meeting:

> It was obvious that [she felt] she could not talk about her mother because if she would, she would be talking against her in a critical manner. She struggles with the idea of them [her brother and she] being unfaithful and untrue to her mother and not appreciating her parents and holding the proper respect for them.
>
> The brother states that the situation has been a bad one all . . . her life. The mother has been very demanding of her and has denied her things which a girl ordinarily would have, and she has punished her frequently and the punishment has been out of proportion to the deed. . . .

When the patient is told that she is called into the office to talk about her mother or parents or brothers, if she so desires, and that her brother has called me, which she requested him to do, and that she may talk if she desires, she talks with a great deal of emotion.

. . . she talks for one hour and fifteen minutes constantly, during which time there are a great many tears and much self-accusation for saying what she does say, and constantly the expression comes, "What will my mother say?"

During this session I told the doctor that I believed that Ma never approved of me or loved me. I just couldn't satisfy her. I desperately wanted her to love me, but I continually disappointed her. I longed to call her "Mother," as American girls did, but she said that was disrespectful and slapped me. I wanted her to call me "honey," which is what my girlfriend's mother called her. But she called me by my name or more often used the Dutch term *meid* (girl); she seldom used the endearing term *meisje* (little girl). I wanted her to tell me I looked nice and to compliment my childish efforts at various things, but she seldom praised me or expressed her approval of what I did. I remember one rare occasion when she did praise me. It was after a Christmas program in which I played, without error, an organ-piano duet with my piano teacher. Ma complimented me because I hadn't made any mistakes — which, she had frequently reminded me, she fully expected me to do.

As I struggled to recall my childhood relationship with her, my memories surprised me. I realized that even as a very young child I was afraid of Ma. My biggest fear was that she would reject me, and I believed that she had, that she only tolerated me. Her approval of me was always tied to my being a good girl, and a good girl I was not. Every time I disappointed her, I disliked myself.

Gary Smalley and John Trent, coauthors of *The Blessing: Giving and Gaining Family Approval,* have explained that parents sometimes withhold praise and words of love because they think their children *know* they are loved. Some parents also think that it's possible to praise a child too much: "Telling children their good points is like putting on perfume. A little is OK; but put too much on and it stinks." Smalley and Trent point out that praise for good behavior isn't a bad thing, but that expressions of love and approval shouldn't always be linked to what a child does: "When words of value are only linked to a child's performance, they lose much of their impact." I had gotten very little positive reinforcement from my mother, for good behavior or anything else, and I was beginning to see that I was paying an emotional price for that.

I was also beginning to realize that my mother and I were very much alike in some ways. This was a difficult realization for me, because I hated it when anyone said I was like my mother. My father had sometimes said that Ma and I were very much alike, which explained the tension between us, but I hadn't seen it. My husband had also made this observation on occasion, usually during a particularly tense situation or an argument between us. Does this type of person choose Calvinism, I wondered, or does Calvinism produce this kind of person? (Eventually my appreciation for John Calvin's teachings about the peace and joy of knowing Jesus replaced the mistaken notions of my childhood.)

I began to see that I had many of my mother's traits — and I didn't like it. Like her, I am tidy — although as a child I wasn't. In fact, Ma was compulsive about neatness. That's probably why she gave me so many "tidying" tasks: I often straightened out her fruit cellar, the basement, her sewing cabinet, and drawers, cupboards, and shelves. Occasionally she expressed her appreciation, but she was never tolerant of my sloppiness. Sometimes I would call downstairs from my bedroom, "Ma, I can't find my slip and I don't have any more," or "Ma, I can't find any more hankies." It hurt when she would come upstairs, with some special radar find the wayward articles, and say, "Heh, *sloddervos* [sloppy one], why don't you keep your clothes neat?"

I am also self-disciplined, as Ma was — although again, as a child, I was the opposite. Now I seldom postpone unpleasant tasks, preferring to finish the most difficult and distasteful ones first, but back then I put play and pleasure before work. To me, summer was for reading and rocking in the swing on our screened porch, hitting the house on the backward arc. The thump, thump, thump against the wall would get Ma's attention, and she would call from the kitchen, "Have you made the beds yet?" Of course I hadn't made the beds yet. Why should I make the boys' beds, I would think, when they're outdoors playing? Aloud I would say — though not loud enough for Ma to hear — "I'm going."

But by then she would have come to the porch and torn the book out of my hands. She wouldn't return it until later, when I had finished all my work, or sometimes not until the next day.

Ma was convinced that a woman's role was homemaking, and so she tried to teach me some of the "feminine" fine arts. I did learn to sew and made some of my clothes while I was in high school. But I didn't like knitting and tatting, and I didn't apply myself to learning them. Ma and I would frequently argue over this, and she would slap me. She was baffled by my inability — or stubborn unwillingness, as she saw it — to learn or do certain things. Why did her daughter refuse to acquire some of the skills she would need as a woman? For years she kept the drunken weave of my first attempt at knitting (I was nine then), to show my children, she threatened, how clumsy

I was. She had learned to knit when she was six or seven, she said. During World War I, when she was a young girl, she had made mittens for soldiers.

Pa said that Ma loved me, that she just wanted me to learn how to be a good wife and mother. That seemed like malarkey to me. She *said* that motherhood was life's most fulfilling role, but she didn't seem to enjoy it. Could my mother have been frustrated, even depressed? I don't know. But if she was, small wonder that she had trouble coping with a daughter who may already have been suffering from depression in childhood.

I cowered under Ma's disapproval and discipline, whether it was physical or verbal. I learned to lie, sometimes deftly, most often clumsily. And I was beginning to realize that my guilt over my lies was now haunting me.

Easy Way Out

A lying tongue hates those it hurts.

Proverbs 26:28

MA ALWAYS SAID it was easier to tell the truth and get the trouble over with, but I never quite believed her. Lies sometimes spared me her punishment.

Lying is sin — I knew that. But sometimes I felt there was no other alternative. If I told the truth about something and it displeased Ma, she would slap me or whip me. When Ma would catch me in a lie, she would be furious. Lying violated the fifth commandment, and she couldn't stand that. "You never learn until it hurts you," she would say when she punished me for lying. But the pain didn't help.

Whenever Ma caught me in a lie, she would tell Pa. That would disappoint him, and I hated disappointing Pa, but even the prospect of letting him down didn't keep me from lying when I thought it might work. I would squirm when he would tell me that he wished I wouldn't give Ma so much trouble, and I always promised him I would try to be better. If only I could have acted more like Ma's definition of a girl; if only I wouldn't have talked back, read too much, been so sloppy. . . . Then I wouldn't have had to lie so often, and Pa would have been much happier with me.

Frequently I would plan to lie. I would decide quite deliberately which would be worse: admitting the truth and accepting the punishment, or planning a foolproof (so I thought) lie that would spare me Ma's disapproval. Whenever I chose to lie, my guilt multiplied deep inside me. Years later, I was beginning to realize that I had stored all that guilt — and that now it was beginning to attack me. Maybe that's why God seemed so far away from me in the hospital — I felt far away from him because my past sins had now caught up with me.

I could write about many of my lies. But there are two incidents in particular, widely separated in time, that show why I sometimes chose to lie in spite of my ambivalent feelings about doing so.

When I was in the third grade, I told a very big lie. It was the first day after Christmas vacation, and I had been exuberant all morning. Friends at school who didn't go to my church would notice that I was wearing nail polish for the first time — natural transparent color — and my new boots. These weren't old-fashioned galoshes with buckles; these were real boots. True, they didn't have zippers like the more expensive boots, but they did have snap buttons, which were much nicer than buckles. Ma had remembered I wanted the new style, even though she believed the old-fashioned kind were warmer over the ankle and much more practical.

After showing off, I placed my boots under my desk proudly. I felt like I belonged because my boots were like everybody else's. Recess came. Boots on. Recess ended. Boots off. Safely.

But after the lunch bell rang, my world fell apart. I pushed my books, papers, and pencil into my desk, and grabbed one of my boots — the one for my left foot. I pulled it on hard, and to my horror a semicircle of rubber — about the size of a silver dollar — came off the top as I tugged. I was shocked and terrified.

My hunger was gone. I loitered until my teacher, Miss T., comforted me and then gently pushed me out of the classroom. How could I tell Ma? I hoped she wouldn't notice, but I started to plan a way to pacify her in case she did.

It didn't help that by the time I got home, I was late for lunch. We had bread and hot chocolate, one of my favorites, but I couldn't eat. Ma looked at me curiously. Two small vertical creases crossed the beginning of the wrinkles on her forehead. "Why don't you eat?"

"I'm not hungry."

"What's the matter? What happened?" She looked at the boys, but they said nothing because they knew nothing.

After the meal Ma prayed, and I tried to hurry out of the house. But Ma was suspicious, and she watched me closely. The way I pulled on my boots was a giveaway.

"*Pas op!* [Be careful!]" she said. "You'll tear them." And then she saw the already torn spot. Instantly she was angry.

"How did you do that? How? How?" My brothers watched.

My carefully planned lie came out awkwardly. "I didn't."

"You didn't? Didn't? Look at that hole. It didn't fall out!"

"I didn't do it," I repeated stubbornly.

"If you didn't do it, then who did?" She jerked my arm, wildly and tightly, stood me up straight, and forced my eyes to meet hers by pinching my chin in two fingers and lifting my head roughly.

"I didn't, Ma. The DeBoer boy did it!" I was miserable. Jack sat behind me in school, and I talked about him frequently, sometimes exaggerating his misbehavior, which was actually no worse than mine.

"I can't understand it," Ma snorted. "What was the teacher doing? Did you tell her? He'll have to pay for it — a pair of new boots wrecked by monkey business." My fear increased as her fury mounted.

"He couldn't help it, Ma. I know he couldn't. And the teacher didn't see it." I didn't want my beloved teacher caught in my mess.

Ma grabbed the stick she always kept handy in a corner of the kitchen but held off hitting me with it. "You'll have to tell the principal. Don't come home until you tell him."

At that I burst into tears. I couldn't sustain the lie any more. "I did it myself, Ma. The DeBoer boy didn't do it. I did it. I couldn't help it."

My deceit made her even angrier, and she whipped me, hard. When I got back to school after lunch, my teacher asked why my eyes were red, but I didn't tell her. I didn't know whether I felt worse about the pain of the whipping or my boots, but my guilt bothered me more than both. I knew what sin was, and I had sinned — again.

For a short while this punishment and the guilt I felt kept me from lying, but eventually I went back to my deceptive behavior. More often than not my desire to win Ma's approval won out over the importance of telling the truth.

Much later, when I was seventeen or eighteen, I lied about attending my first movie. By then, most of my friends were attending movies, but my parents still wouldn't allow my brothers and me to go to the theater. Once in a while Ma allowed us to go to movies at the local museum on Saturday afternoons. We walked four miles there and four miles back to see Rin Tin Tin. But Hollywood movies were from the devil, Ma said.

The movie I wanted to see — *Gone with the Wind* — was showing at the Majestic Theater, a place of sin. "Can't I go just this once?" I begged Ma. "Everybody else is going." That wasn't true. But Ma was adamant; movies are sin, and that's that. If Jesus were to come, would I want to be sitting in that theater?

But I disobeyed. I shivered as I paid my quarter for admission. I had read the book twice (also forbidden), weeping much of the time, torn between wishing I could be as sweet and true as Melanie and wishing that I could be as desirable as Scarlett so that a swashbuckler like Rhett Butler would sweep me into his arms.

I went to the theater with three of my friends. We were positive our sin would be found out. I watched the movie with a horrified fascination. Even the sinning in it was beautiful — and followed by awful destruction. When Atlanta burned, one of my friends and I felt the theater was burning just as hard, and we hoped Jesus wouldn't come — at least not until the movie was finished. I knew I would never be myself again, but I didn't quite know how I had changed.

My close friend ended up telling her mother all about it, and she listened carefully. The two of them actually discussed it together. I fantasized that I would tell Ma about the movie and that maybe she and I would talk about it. But my fantasy didn't come true. When I told her, she was speechless. She looked at me in horror, not responding to my "Say something, Ma." She started crying and kept on crying. For three days she cried whenever she saw me. A whipping would have been easier for me.

After that I still did go to movies occasionally, but I never told Ma about it again. Dealing with the guilt of lying to her was easier than enduring the pain I had seen in her face when I had been honest. Her grief had stunned me.

These two incidents illustrate the gulf that often separated

Ma and me. Perhaps she and I were alike in many ways, but we had differences too. She never understood me, and I never understood her, even though we both tried hard in our own way. Good communication between two people occurs when the receiver understands what the sender said and intended. Had Ma and I ever really communicated? Not often. Recognizing this was difficult, but it was something I could build on in my therapy.

Too often in communicating with each other we fail to allow for a margin of error. As a child I didn't realize this, and I'm sure Ma didn't, either. It never occurred to me then that part of the difficulty between Ma and me may simply have been that she was a "foreigner" trying to talk to me in English. Some of the time she may have misspoken herself and not clarified what she meant because she didn't like to repeat things. Another thing I didn't realize as a child was that communication involves give-and-take. It never occurred to me that Ma — an adult, my mother — had needs just like I did. Kathie Carlson, the author of *In Her Image: The Unhealed Daughter's Search for Her Mother*, comments on this phenomenon:

[The child's perspective] does not see the mother in herself, as a person with her own needs, interests, and concerns separate from the child. Nor does it take into account important factors affecting the mother's life and ability to parent, factors such as economics, what kinds of support the mother herself had available, what her own experience of being mothered was. It also overlooks the effects that cultural expectations and stereotypes of mothers have on the mother's parenting. . . . And finally, the child's perspective envisions the mother inhumanly, assumes she is somehow "matched" to the daughter's need, does not have needs of her own that conflict with her daughter's, and has nearly infinite resources.

In fact, as Charles Allen points out in *God's Psychiatry: Healing of the Mind and Soul,* the child deifies the parent: "The parent is to the child its first God. . . . The parents are the greatest social influence in the life of the child." It is natural for a child to have these great expectations, but they can be very difficult for a parent to handle.

Maybe Ma needed my emotional support as much as I needed her approval. How sad that we missed each other. And what were the implications of this for my role as a mother? If Ma and I were so much alike, would I be able to communicate well with my three daughters?

During my illness I learned that message sending and receiving is an art, and distortions by the sender or the receiver can lead to disaster. Pa often tried to soften Ma's harsh words. "Ma doesn't always say it just right," he would tell me. "Take her for what she means, not for what she says." But it seemed to me that what she *meant* was even worse than her scolding or her whipping. Ma just didn't like me, I decided. Even though I was her only daughter, I was her "ugly duckling."

My doctor and I spent several sessions talking about Ma. Each time I left his office, I thought of more incidents to talk about. I also began to see the kind of child I had been, and I berated myself more and more. No wonder Ma couldn't love me. But what shocked me was the explosive declaration I eventually made: "Well, I hate her too!" After I blurted that out, I shook convulsively and cried; my doctor sat quietly by. He gave me some tissues, and as I wiped my face, he asked, "Do you really hate her?"

I didn't reply.

"If you do, then why does this hurt you so much? Behavior like your mother's only hurts when it comes from people we love very much."

Exhausted, I returned to my room to think about what I had done.

The doctor made these comments after the fifth session in which I talked about Ma:

After one and a quarter hours of talking about her mother's insistence on having things done the way she wants them, and the mother's having denied the girl various things, such as dates, clothing, and education, because she was a girl and the boys should have that, she feels very guilty. She feels as though she has turned on her mother and has been unfaithful to her. She is made to see things in a somewhat different light by the time that she leaves the office.

She is told, however, that she is not to go to her mother's home on Sunday and the holiday [Memorial Day], as is planned. She feels that the mother will make a terrific rumpus about having the plans called off. Nevertheless, the situation is left that she must not go home to her parents this long weekend. She may take a ride with her husband on Saturday afternoon. She may go to her husband's parents' home on Sunday afternoon and stay there overnight and return on the afternoon of the next day, which is a holiday. She does not like to accept this but does so and says that she realizes she cannot go to her mother's house.

The Core of the Matter

Have thine own way, Lord! Have thine own way!
Search me and try me, Master, today.
Open mine eyes, my sin show me now,
as in thy presence humbly I bow.

Have thine own way, Lord! Have thine own way!
Hold o'er my being absolute sway.
Fill with thy Spirit till all shall see
Christ only, always, living in me.

"Have Thine Own Way, Lord,"
stanzas 2, 4

THE PREVIOUS therapy session had been unnerving. I was still stunned that I had said that I hated my mother. After all, I wasn't a rambunctious teenager longing to burst the bonds of dependence. I was a "mature" Christian. I couldn't believe that such feelings roiled inside me and that they had shot up and out of me like a geyser. Could a *Christian* daughter speak that way about a Christian mother? I was wicked, ugly. Still, although I usually felt like the apostle Peter, often blurting out my thoughts before thinking them through and then wanting to take my words back, this time I didn't. The rock was still there inside me, yet in some ways it had been dislodged a bit. It both hurt and helped me that I had talked so frankly about my mother. An indefinable mixture of heaviness and lightness stirred within me, a touch of hope.

By external standards, Ma was a good mother. So, if I could become so messed up with a good mother, how would my children survive with a bad mother — a mother who even had to be confined for several months in a mental hospital? Wasn't it better, then, to have my children brought up by other people? Maybe I would never be able to care for them. For the first time I recognized that my thoughts were unhealthy, sick.

My doctor helped me to see that after achieving this first milestone — admitting that I was sick, unable to cure myself, and in need of help — I would have to continue examining my childhood in order to make more progress. Alfred Sloat, author of *Strangers and Comrades,* has commented that "[it's] a lot easier to shape the course of a river with your fingers than to shape people." Yet my mother had shaped me. The problem was that I couldn't live with the shape. Personalities and life views are to a great extent formed during childhood, my doctor explained. I had to examine and relive how, as a child, I had responded to Ma, especially during the times that were most painful for me. We spent many therapy sessions on this topic.

I grew up believing that I was a Christian only when I worked hard (no matter what I was doing) and when I obeyed (not only Ma but any authority). Ma punished me to teach me these lessons. I wasn't a "nice little girl," Ma said often. I didn't have domestic interests, and my desire for knowledge and longing for answers disturbed her. "Boys don't like smart girls," she explained, "so stop acting smart." She accused me of wanting to learn the wrong things — not what girls should learn — and said that boys were much easier to raise. Rightly or wrongly, I translated Ma's discipline and disapproval to mean that she was disappointed with her only daughter.

I rarely pleased Ma, even after I was an adult. I could not — and that was my failing — give her what she wanted most: the gift of intimacy. She wanted her daughter to be an extension of herself, and I couldn't be that, partly because I was terrified of being that. In *In Her Image: The Unhealed Daughter's Search for Her Mother*, Kathie Carlson calls this matrophobia. She defines this as "a fear of being 'just like her,' a predominant fear among women in our society that sometimes is surrounded with dread and despair." I wanted so much to be free to be myself.

When Ray and I left for Nigeria, I knew our going displeased Ma because she and Pa had just built a house a few blocks from ours and had joined our church.

With my doctor's help, I began to acknowledge the mountains of anger I had accumulated over the years. Unresolved pain, hurts, and anger had developed into the psychological cancer that was now eating away at me.

Once I had started talking to him about my childhood, I found continuing less difficult. (I didn't want Ma to know, however, and whenever I saw her, I felt sad.) It took a while for me to believe that Ma had been unfair to me, but gradually I came to that realization as I relived many incidents in my childhood that had invited Ma's disapproval by word, slap, stick, or silence.

The older I got, the more stunningly appropriate Ma's discipline became. I remember an incident that happened when I was in the sixth grade. One evening when Ma said good night to me, she noticed that I was chewing gum. "Spit your gum out, *meid*," she said to me. "Otherwise it will get stuck in the bed."

"Yes, Ma."

But just as quickly I forgot, and I failed to dispose of my Black Jack before I fell asleep. The next morning I noticed out of the corner of my first open eye a small black spider on my pillow. I shuddered, pulled away, and saw another spider on the sheet. My hand flew to my mouth; my gum was gone.

My fear of spiders grew into my fear of Ma's wrath. Maybe she wouldn't find out if I made my bed right away. Afterward I went slowly to the kitchen for breakfast. But I wasn't going to escape.

"What's that in your hair, *meid?*" Ma greeted me, grasping a tuft of my hair.

"What?" I asked, knowing.

"How do you think I'll get that gum out, *kind* [child]?" Without another word, she got the scissors and cut two big hanks of hair close to my scalp. She left two circles, bigger than half-dollars, of very short hair on my head, like two patches of dead grass marring a healthy lawn. At school, when my classmates made fun of me, I wanted to run away. I didn't want to come back until my hair filled in.

I remember too a wool jacket I got as a Christmas present when I was sixteen. It was a beautiful plaid of brown, beige, and orange. I liked it and so did my friends. One afternoon in March a friend and I decided to walk home from high school. The day was sunny but windy and cold. Our three-mile route home took us across an overpass above the train yards, and we decided to look over the railing to see what trains looked like from overhead. Just as we did, WHOOSH — an engine sent up a billow of smoke that caught us both. Our hair, our faces, our jackets — all were black, black, black. Only our teeth and our eyes were white. When we looked at each other, we burst into gales of laughter, and we kept laughing as we sauntered home.

But as I got close to my house, my mood changed. My beautiful jacket was now filthy, and Ma wouldn't see the humor in what had happened. I thought of every excuse I could, but the evidence of what I had done was obvious. Ma was furious, just as I thought she'd be. "You just aren't worth anything good," Ma said — something she'd said to me many times before. "It costs money to get a jacket dry cleaned."

I had a date that night, and I was grateful that she didn't ground me. But the punishment she gave me was almost as bad. She said I would have to wear the jacket, and that I couldn't wash my hair. (She said she wouldn't let me wash it because I would catch a cold, but that wasn't true. We didn't have a hair dryer, but I could have dried my hair over the floor register.) I was mortified. I cleaned as much of the soot out of my hair as I could with a washcloth, then covered it with a hat. Next I put on warm clothes, including an extra wool sweater. Immediately after my date arrived, we left. When we were just outside the door, I threw my jacket into the bushes near the house. "It's so warm," I told him. I didn't want him to know what I or my mother had done. What would people say?

It took me a long time to recognize that I was fostering an illusion that in Christian families all is ideal. With my doctor's help, I saw that I, like my mother, protected this illusion, fearing, just as much as she did, "what people would say." I began to grasp the fact that even though both Ma and I were Christians, something had damaged our relationship badly.

Part of the problem, I began to see, was my conscience. My doctor explained that conscience is a mysterious part of us — born in us, yes, but very much formed by our parents, our church, and our teachers. My mother had shaped my conscience with her ideas about religion, Sabbath observance, work, obedience, femaleness, and maleness. She taught me exactly as she had been taught by her mother. Things might have been different if she had had four girls and one boy instead of four boys and one girl. Or if she had had more education. Or if she had been born in America. Or if she had been able to adapt better to American life instead of fearing it and building a fortress around her family. If. If. If. No mother can be everything to her children.

Not only had Ma shaped my strong conscience, but she had also taught me not to sin against it. I had always believed that her conscience was stronger than mine. And yet her conscience was so rule-bound — and didn't Scripture warn Christians about that? I saw that I had to examine many of the do's and don'ts that governed my conscience.

My doctor agreed. The time had come, he said, for me to search the Bible for myself and reform my conscience. I had to become me instead of a dual person wanting to be both a mother-approved daughter and an independent adult with separate interests and goals. This would require time, effort, and therapy.

As I write this story, I'm reading *The Dance of Anger: A Woman's Guide to Changing the Patterns of Intimate Relationships* by Harriet Goldhar Lerner. Her definition of what she calls "deselfing" makes me realize that my relationship with my mother had deselfed me:

> *Deselfing* means that too much of one's self (including one's thoughts, wants, beliefs, and ambitions) is "negotiable" under pressures from the relationship.
>
> Even when the person doing the most compromising of self is not aware of it, deselfing takes its inevitable toll.
>
> The partner who is doing the most sacrificing of self

stores up the most repressed anger and is especially vulnerable to becoming depressed and developing other emotional problems. She (and in some cases he) may end up in a therapist's office, or even in a medical or psychiatric hospital, saying, "What is wrong with me?" rather than asking, "What is wrong with this relationship?"

Ma had not hurt me on purpose, but hearts are not chalkboards from which pain can easily be erased at the end of the day, whether that pain was intentionally inflicted or not. All I knew as a child was that she expected me to obey, immediately and without question, and when I didn't, I bore the consequences.

I had indeed absorbed most of Ma's rigid, legalistic rules and ideas. I didn't want to be like her, yet it seemed that what I hadn't learned from her personally I had inherited from her genetically. Her teachings had become the warp and woof of my living style. But now I had to make my own choices, my own decisions about what to believe and how to live. Kathie Carlson explains what I was dealing with during my illness: "What a daughter needs . . . is permission and support to separate from her mother: to accomplish on her own, to make her own mistakes and have her triumphs, and to be as different from her mother as her own personality and inner patterns direct her to be."

If, during the first several years of my marriage to Ray, someone had accused me of being tied to my mother's apron strings, I would have scoffed. And so far as I knew I would have been speaking honestly. I was independent, living in another city, and working. Ma disapproved of my working, of course. Husbands brought home the potatoes, she said, and wives cooked them.

I had fooled myself into believing that I was not a deselfed woman.

Some might say, "Surely as an adult you could have changed the relationship between you and your mother." A woman with more inner spiritual strength than I possessed may well have been able to do so, with the help of the Holy Spirit, and that would indeed be a blessing. But I couldn't, and I had to face my inability to do so. The fallenness of human beings is a fact; we aren't able to be the kind of persons we would like to be. My mother, I knew, couldn't change, and I chose not to burden her with my complaints. Changing was my task, I decided, and mine alone.

I reviewed my problems and reduced them to three principal things that were gnawing at me: my relationship with my mother; my belief that today's women, considering the modern conveniences they have access to, should do more for God's kingdom than housework; and my lack of higher education as it affected my self-esteem. I started fighting with the misguided ideas I had on these topics, and that was a sign of progress.

In my next therapy session I talked about my ideas about work in God's kingdom. My doctor made these notes on our conversation:

> Once again she expresses the opinion, as she frequently has before, that she doubts her motives in doing whatever she may have done. Her reasoning is that if she did things, such as going to school, becoming a secretary, being efficient, being meticulous, etc., because she had to satisfy her own selfish [needs] and guilt feelings, then her motives were not of a very high order and ought to be condemned. . . .
>
> She said she didn't know that she had these sort[s] of feelings, or this kind of makeup, except that she realizes now she always had to do things as best that she could and frequently the best wasn't good enough. It becomes very clear that she is struggling with an intense desire to use what

knowledge, ability, and talents she may have in the business world, and the field of missions, or in writing, on the one hand, as over against her responsibility which she knows she has of being a housewife and mother. She asks how much of her time must she give to her family, and not the question one would like to hear, which is — how can she give . . . her entire time to her family and do it with pleasure and a sense of accomplishment.

For the time being she gets a great deal of comfort and obvious satisfaction out of a simple remark which is that to be a mother and housewife is one of the most honored and greatest occupations that an individual can possibly have. She has had this same reaction before, and it does not last. The obvious fact of the matter is that this woman would like to [give] a good deal of her time over to work other than doing housework and taking care of the children, and would especially like to direct that time to writing and doing missionary work.

My doctor was right about my mixed feelings about being a mother and a homemaker. I didn't particularly like housework, but I enjoyed having a clean house. I did tire of tending my four little children, but I loved them dearly. I tried hard to be honest. But did I have to feel so guilty about these admissions?

Why, I wondered, was I so often restless about my role as a woman? I knew the biblical texts commending contentment: "Godliness with contentment is great gain" (1 Tim. 6:6), and "I have learned to be content whatever the circumstances" (Phil. 4:11). Now I was learning to phrase this second text a bit differently: "I have learned to be content *in* whatever circumstances I am" (NASB, my emphasis). My doctor pointed out that to be *content in* is not the same as to be *content with*. I could be *content in* my role as wife and mother, but that didn't mean I had to be content *with it* — forever! In no way should this text stifle any goals I wished to set for myself. One little word was different, but what a difference in meaning it made. It opened new vistas for me later.

I liked the other roles I had been able to play in Nigeria. I loved working on the mission field. I enjoyed keeping the mission books (using the British monetary system of pounds, shillings, and pence). I took satisfaction in teaching Sunday School, writing articles, and corresponding with many people. And I liked the assistance I got with my more traditional duties. I enjoyed having most of the daily housework done by the servants, and I appreciated the relief when one of them took care of my children for a few hours.

I was confused. My doctor and I had established that Nigeria was not the cause of my illness, so that experience seemed within God's will. Still, my doctor continued to suggest that my calling as mother and wife was not only the world's most noble calling but also apparently a woman's only calling. Looking back, I think this particular idea of his had a great deal to do with the times. My illness and therapy preceded the era of the women's movement. On more than one occasion my doctor said, "Lil, psychiatry is quite new. If I were to work with you ten or twenty years from now, my approach might be entirely different." I think he was right — I think that if he had treated me later, he would have developed a broader concept of woman's role than he possessed at this time. And I remain grateful to him for all the positive seeds he planted, some of which didn't blossom until many years later, and some of which continue to blossom today.

I felt torn. I was beginning to realize that, indeed, I did love my family. My children were God's children, and when I was well I would care for them gladly. But was "woman's work" biblically *limited* to bearing and raising children, raising daughters who in turn would bear and raise their own children? I tried to figure out why my desire to do more than this seemed to me to be more selfish and sinful than stewardly and service-oriented. I was happy with and grateful for my family and my role as mother, yet I desired further education and opportunity. No one understood my restlessness, and I didn't, either. I must have sounded quite ridiculous to my doctor: here I was, hospitalized, unable to care for my husband or my children — or myself, for that matter — and I was fixated on other tasks I wanted to undertake. He made these notes about our session:

> Her most frequent self-accusation is that she is now convinced that her desire to [do more than housework and care for her family] is sinful and always has been, and again [she] describes it as mere self-gratification, making her deserving of nothing less than a good deal of guilt and shame for her downright, deliberate sin.
>
> On the other hand, she again states that she realizes that the difficulty she is having is due to illness and she is willing to recognize this. But she struggles with the idea that this started when she was a child, and she feels she has been responsible all the time for the things she has done with her sinful motivation.
>
> She claims she wants to take care of her family and is able to do it as far as she knows, but at the present time she doubts whether her judgment on anything is right.

My doctor understood my thoughts and motives much better than I did, and I relied heavily on his gentle guidance and subtle prodding.

I think it would have helped me to know that I wasn't alone in feeling this way. But I underwent this therapy during the 1950s, a decade before I learned that other Christian women experienced the same unrest that I did. Recently — in 1990 — Mary Stewart Van Leeuwen published a book entitled *Gender and Grace,* in which she articulates the predicament that I was experiencing but couldn't formulate:

> Christians believe in the uniqueness of each individual life. . . . But until recently this was a belief that was regularly qualified the moment a baby girl was born. When a boy was born, few people presumed to predict what kind of work he would be doing thirty years down the road. His options were considered numerous, limited only by his intelligence, motivation and (ideally) the kind of call God issued. But when it came to girls, many Christian parents forgot about created uniqueness, and about Pentecost and its implications. They assumed and even prayed for a successful career as wife and mother, and nothing else. Indeed, some still assume that God, by definition, can call their daughters to nothing else, and that to be single and female (or married, female and not a full-time homemaker) is somehow to have failed, morally and spiritually.

This is a perfect description of what I struggled with in the fifties. The church as well as society, my doctor as well as my mother, believed that being a wife and a mother was a woman's only role and her total role. I stopped arguing with my doctor, because I thought he must be right and I must be wrong.

* * *

Almost five months had passed since I had been admitted to the hospital. My thoughts still caused me pain and made me feel angry. The specific cause of these feelings had begun to take shape. I felt cheated, deprived, robbed of my "self-ness."

I was not *me*. I wanted to tear off the label that said "Made by Ma." I felt like a product.

I felt like a limp onion from which my doctor was peeling every layer of limitation, motivation, self-deceit, pretense, and coverup. The removal of each layer was excruciating. The core of me now lay naked, exposed. At this point in my therapy my primary reaction was how sinful I felt before a righteous and almighty God. The core of me, I thought, wasn't worth saving. But God used my doctor, my pastor, and my husband to convince me otherwise.

"You can't help being ill," said my doctor, "but you can choose how you respond to it, whether it will make you bitter or better, whether you will be victim or victor."

To be a victor, I would have to rebuild my life, separate myself completely from Ma, become totally independent from her, accepting and appreciating her good qualities but discarding those ideas of hers that had crippled me.

Recovery, with the help of others, now became my full-time assignment.

Beginning

You have the true and perfect gentleness.
You have no harshness and no bitterness.
Lord, grant to {me} the grace in you {I} see
that we may live in perfect unity.

"I Greet My Sure Redeemer," stanza 4

MY WILL WAS beginning to function, and I wanted to get better. When people are overweight, they know they ought to lose weight . . . and usually they want to. But they also know they have to *do* something: eat less and exercise regularly. So it is with regaining mental health. One has to learn and practice the principles of mental health when the will has healed enough to share in the therapy.

With my doctor's permission, I retrieved my Bible from m dresser drawer. I still had an annoying tendency to see only t condemning texts rather than the texts of love, encourageme challenge, and, most of all, promise. But I was making progr I struggled with how I perceived and how I practiced forgiver

and I prayed much about my anger, focused now on Ma. I had always been a student of the Bible, but I had looked for the *magic* that would help me forgive any perceived wrong. I told God again and again that I had forgiven Ma because he had forgiven my sins and remembered them no more (Heb. 8:12). But still, I concentrated on my pain. What I began to realize was that forgiveness was not a garment tucked into my dresser drawer, waiting for me to use it; it was a process. Forgiving was something I would have to do over time. And I found that gradually I could forgive specific wrongs against me.

As I gained a better understanding of freedom, liberation, and redemption through Christ's life, death, and resurrection, I was able to let go of my anger against Ma. I realized that although Christ died once to forgive my sins, his action covers yesterday, today, and tomorrow, and God *keeps on* forgiving. Because I "miss the mark" again and again, his forgiveness covers tomorrow as well. Recognizing this helped me to forgive Ma again and again as I felt her continuing disapproval of me.

Belief in this freedom marked the beginning of change in me. Although I had believed I was "born again," that had been something I knew in my head. Now I believed it in my heart as well; I felt it. Knowledge and faith, although both were weak, gave me a way to cope. I gained insight into who I was and how I was formed. I began to understand my conscience, my personality, and my behavior.

Practically speaking, it makes more sense to forgive than to harbor anger. Anger belongs only to its possessor and is usually a liability. Forgiveness healed my emotional pain and helped me wrest control from the people I was forgiving — Ma in particular. One of the things I had to recognize and accept was that forgiveness doesn't change the person being forgiven. Even though I was changing, Ma wasn't going to change. I had to recognize that I would continue to be hurt

and continue to feel inadequate if I allowed Ma's sameness to govern me. But understanding the limits of forgiveness released me from the bondage of Ma's control.

I thought of "confronting" (I dislike that word) my mother, but I decided against it. My doctor had suggested I do this. And certain readers might point to the "advice" of Matthew 5:23-24: "When you are offering your gift at the altar, if you remember that your brother or sister has something against you, leave your gift there before the altar and go; first be reconciled to your brother or sister, and then come and offer your gift" (NRSV). Still, I didn't think it was best to "have it out" with Ma. She hadn't intentionally hurt me, and she was old now. It seemed to me that to burden her with accusations at this stage in her life would be cruel. I had been able, through grace alone, to forgive any perceived wrongs. I decided that my reasons for not confronting her may have been wrong, but that my motivation was not.

"*Ja, meid,*" she said to me one day, reverting to the way she had addressed me in my childhood, "my friends all say you have changed."

"Yes, Ma, I have," I replied. "I'm grown up now, and I've also grown in Christ. Most of all I'm learning what he wants me to be."

Ma didn't understand — I don't think she could have. Of course, she didn't know that I had forgiven her, because she didn't know that she had hurt me. It helped me to recognize that she and I were both God's children, and that I needed to love her and accept her as my sister in Christ. In *The Christian Looks at Himself,* Anthony Hoekema makes this point by paraphrasing the apostle Paul: "Now, says Paul, we are to accept one another as Christ has accepted us; not on the basis of merit, not because we like one [person] better than another . . . but simply because we are in Christ together."

I began to think about leaving the hospital, at first with reluctance and then with determination. Both my doctor and my husband encouraged me. I was sleeping better, and I was experiencing less anxiety and fewer panic attacks. Weekends were going much better, too. I was able to visit not only with Ray's parents but also with my own. There were things to look forward to "on the outside": the mission board had given Ray and me permission to live in one of the houses it kept for missionaries on furlough, and my doctor promised that I could have the children home one at a time. This prospect was wonderful — but also challenging and scary.

Another four weeks remained before my doctor discharged me. Many people think that discharge from the hospital means that the patient is well. Believe me, it doesn't. It is simply another beginning. Facing the world outside the hospital is a new challenge to be met — one that frightened me.

I continued my therapy. Even though I was making progress, I often whined, "I'm not getting better. I'll never get better." My doctor would say, "You're not looking back far enough. Ask yourself if you're better than you were when we talked for the first time. You can't expect to redo in a few short months what took a lifetime to build."

I had so much to unlearn. My first task was to stop being so hard on myself. I had to use my new insights to rebuild myself in all kinds of ways. To learn how to respond to my mother without allowing her to control me. To allow myself pleasurable feelings. To identify my own (not others') values. To be satisfied with less than perfection. To allow myself to be needy. To stop measuring myself by what others thought of me. My doctor and I talked about growth in holiness and spiritual outlook through the Holy Spirit. I recognized and accepted the challenge.

Yes, my doctor assured me, my brokenness would heal,

but the wounds would remain tender for a long time. These wounds were deep; some would cause me trouble occasionally, maybe even for the rest of my life. My relationship with Ma would be an ongoing struggle. My doctor explained that if I pleased Ma simply to win her approval, I would be allowing her to control me. She then would determine my self-esteem. Loving her was different from seeking her approval. And loving her involved making a decision to love her, whether or not she was lovable or even likeable. This is the kind of love that M. Scott Peck describes in *The Road Less Traveled*:

> Genuine love is volitional rather than emotional. The person who truly loves does so because of a decision to love. This person has made a commitment to be loving whether or not the loving feeling is present. If it is, so much the better; but if it isn't, the commitment to love, the will to love, still stands, and is still exercised.

I appreciated my doctor's openness with me; he didn't sugarcoat the future. Although I had been very wary of him when I had first started my therapy, I had come to trust him. He was never aloof or disinterested. He concentrated on helping one muddled young woman try to develop a better self-image and bring balance into her life.

No matter how highly we may regard ourselves, all of us have needs. There's nothing wrong with having these needs, but I hadn't realized this before. Over the years I had built a solid barrier around myself to defend my fragile self-image and to keep other people from seeing my neediness. I had peered at the world through narrow chinks in my fortress, often getting a distorted picture of reality. My elementary teachers had recognized this, the doctor pointed out.

My illness was the complete crumbling of my faulty

defenses. Small wonder I had felt so totally exposed, so defenseless. My fortress had been totally devastated. Now I was no longer putting up walls; I was strengthening myself by working on *me*. By enlisting God's help, and by leaning on my doctor, my minister, and my husband for support, I was beginning to rebuild my life.

I had to answer several questions: Can I change? What will it cost me? How can I do it? What about those things that can't be changed? These are all commonsense questions that require more than commonsense wisdom to answer. I was blessed to have the help of the Bible. As far as my *self* was concerned, I was beginning to get acquainted with the person I wanted to be. I tried to change what I didn't like and accept the rest of me.

But I also had to accept what I couldn't change. "Don't expect to change your mother," my doctor said. "Don't expect her to change herself, either. Don't expect to change anyone; learn to accept people as they are, bad points as well as good points. If anyone is going to change, it will have to be you." That truth still helps me today. It's a hard truth, but an important one.

Scott Peck begins *The Road Less Traveled* with one of these hard truths:

> Life is difficult.
>
> This is a great truth, one of the greatest truths. It is a great truth because once we truly see this truth, we transcend it. Once we truly know that life is difficult — once we truly understand and accept it — then life is no longer difficult. Because once it is accepted, the fact that life is difficult no longer matters.

The psalmist adds divine comfort: "You [God] hem me in — behind and before; you have laid your hand upon me. Such knowledge is too wonderful for me" (Ps. 139:5-6). Never before had I seen the beauty of that text. If God is behind and before me and has laid his hand on me, truly there is nothing to fear. God is not unfair, as I had sometimes fearfully thought, but life is. Now I was learning that even when life is unfair, God is there.

If I couldn't expect others to change to accommodate what I would have liked them to be, my biggest challenge now was changing me. One of the major drawbacks I faced was that I hadn't been raised to see things as they were. My upbringing — at home, at school, at church — had taught me that life is either black or white, with no gray areas. Experience didn't verify that concept, of course; I saw gray, never complete whiteness or total blackness. But my mind told me that wasn't possible. I was trapped by the contradiction between what I believed and what I experienced.

No one had ever corrected my absolutist interpretation of "Be ye perfect, even as your Father in heaven is perfect." God knows that none of us can be perfect. Yet I had been unable to accept the wounds dealt me by other Christians, whose arrows are often very sharp, and my own perfectionism had almost killed me. I knew but hadn't experienced the truth that God himself perfected our imperfections and purified our impurities when he sent his only Son to shed his blood to re-create us, to make us into new people. Paul explained it so well: "I have been crucified with Christ and I no longer live, but Christ lives in me. The life I live in the body, I live by faith in the Son of God, who loved me and gave himself for me" (Gal. 2:20).

Now I saw that the distortion of sin is part of this broken world, a world that only God can repair. I saw that God is gracious, merciful. He has provided a new way. Why had I not *learned* this as a child?

I realized now that I hadn't accepted any part of myself

because every part of me was imperfect. Because I hadn't been able to come to terms with my imperfection, because I hadn't been able to bend, not even a little, I broke. *This was the root cause of much of my depression.* All the teachings of my deeply religious childhood had made me a legalistic, works-righteous, inflexible Christian. Mine was a life of "You must," "You should," and "If you don't, I'll . . ." I had never experienced the joy that comes from accepting the full cleansing and total pardon of Jesus Christ and the new and free life in him.

I recognized that this new life in Christ wasn't going to work magic. Being right with Jesus didn't mean I wouldn't face any problems or challenges. Life, as Peck says, is difficult. Saved Christians are still flawed Christians. I now saw the world both as it is and as it could be through Christ's redemption and liberation. My illness was making me more tolerant and compassionate — of others and of myself. No person on earth is free of imperfection. Even King David, the man after God's own heart, was a murderer.

These were the kinds of thoughts which signaled that I was beginning to get well. Like a person taking her first few steps after surgery, steadied by the strong arms of others, I had begun my journey down the long road to full recovery.

Although I couldn't detect any change at first, today I can see that God has used my illness to change me dramatically and continually; even today the transformation goes on. I have learned to know God as loving and kind, as the God who gave himself through his Son to redeem and liberate me. The angry God of justice and vengeance, the God of my childhood, has become my Father of love, comfort, and freedom.

Home

{My} protector is the Lord; shade for {me}
    he will afford.
Neither sun nor moon shall smite;
    God shall guard by day and night.
He will ever keep {my} soul; what would harm
    he will control.
In {my} home and by {my} way
God will keep {me} day by day.

"To the Hills I Lift My Eyes,"
stanza 2

A FEW WEEKS before I was discharged, my doctor prescribed an antidepressant drug for me. These drugs are common now, but they were new at the time. This medication reduced my tension and anxiety considerably and consequently helped change how I viewed things. No longer did I see the hospital as my refuge and comfort. When I was out on a pass, I wanted to stay out, and this excited me.

By the time I left the hospital in late July, I had been a patient for almost half a year. I was happy to be discharged.

These are some of the comments my doctor made in his discharge summary:

> A good deal of her difficulty has been that she wanted an education and hasn't had it. This is a constant struggle with her. She realizes this and realizes that she should not try to go to school with the children being the age they are and that they need her care. On the other hand she constantly struggles with the idea that she would like to go to school even now. . . .
>
> She received a few electric shock treatments, but was [mainly] carried along on psychotherapy. She has made rather good strides since she was placed on [medicine]. Her course in the hospital has been up and down. It took a long time for her to admit that it was possible for her to become so sick by reason of emotional difficulty. She wanted to lay it all to the factor of sin. Besides this she accused herself of being stubborn, self-willed and selfish.
>
> At the time of discharge she was much changed. Her problems [were] there but were not as acute and did not bother her all the time. It was possible for her to go without any sleeping medication at all after she was placed on [medicine], and she has noticed calmness.
>
> She is to return at intervals for out-patient psychiatric care.
>
> Final diagnosis: Manic depression, depressed. She probably has had several attacks before.
>
> Discharged as much improved.

Although I was glad to be "out," coming home was like biting into a grapefruit when you expect to bite into an orange

— not as sweet. Even so, the tartness was satisfactory. Most of my personal problems were still unsolved: my ideas about kingdom work, my sense of inferiority, my yearning for education, and my fear of meeting people. But my relationship with my mother wasn't as difficult. I had gained determination and a hint of confidence — which was good, because I would need both. I saw that before I could take care of my children by myself, I would need help. I would also have to face other challenges: picking up the phone when it rang, answering the knock on the door, walking on the street. I shivered just thinking about it. Rebuilding would be hard.

It was a July afternoon when we moved into the mission house. It was clean, bright, cheery, and completely furnished. Ray had stocked the kitchen cupboards, so I wouldn't have to shop right away.

The first couple of days I drew the shades so that no one could see inside. Twice a day I took hurried walks, hoping I wouldn't meet anyone I knew. (I didn't.) I still had depressing thoughts, felt discouraged, and was extremely tired. Everything seemed like a great deal of work — washing the dishes, talking, eating. But now I had the will, weak as it was, to consciously work toward mental health.

If you say you're depressed, well-intentioned people respond with "Stop feeling sorry for yourself" or "Forget about it!" Good advice. But when you suffer from depression, as my doctor pointed out, it's almost impossible to forget. He gave me a helpful suggestion for dealing with the negative thoughts that often obsessed me. "*Substitute* positive thoughts," he said, "beginning with thirty seconds at a time. When you can do that, increase the span to sixty seconds. Keep increasing the time as you get stronger." I practiced this technique religiously. I would call to mind words, scenes, good memories, and lines of hymns, and as I increased the span I could retain positive thoughts, I used Bible texts. I wrote down encouraging lines and verses; scraps of paper with positive ideas littered many parts of the house. I also listened to records and the radio. Even today, I substitute positive ideas when negative thoughts impinge on me.

Eventually I was able to put into practice one of the ideas that Charles Allen suggests in *God's Psychiatry: Healing of the Mind and Soul.* He advises meditating on Psalm 23 five times a day for seven days to help establish a positive pattern of thinking. "The power of this Psalm," he explains, "lies in the fact that it represents a positive, hopeful, faith[full] approach to life." I could use this psalm constructively now only because my doctor and my pastor had prepared my heart for it.

I was slowly improving, but I didn't like it when people asked me how I was doing. I'm sure they expected the casual "Fine" in response, but I wasn't up to it. My doctor kiddingly suggested, "Ask them, 'Do you have an hour? Then I'll try to tell you.'" I never did, of course.

During this time I learned that a few of the articles I had written while Ray and I were in Nigeria had been accepted by three different magazines. This encouraged me. I was also encouraged by the fact that I took care of our baby, Anita, on a few occasions when her foster parents went to church, and I enjoyed it. I thought about going to church myself, but I couldn't face that challenge yet. (It took more than two years before I had enough courage to return to church; I was glad my minister understood my fear.)

Both Ray and I could see that I was making progress. Each night I cooked dinner — a task that once would have completely overwhelmed me. And I dreamed about reuniting our family — a prospect I had once found very daunting.

Ray and I planned to live in the mission house for a few

weeks longer and then move into our own home, which was currently being vacated. (We had sold our house to one of my brothers, and now he had sold it back to us.) Our two oldest children, Ken and Donna, we would bring home one at a time and at two- or three-week intervals, so that by the time school started in September (there was a Christian school nearby), we would be ready to assume a somewhat normal life. I would have help caring for Ken and Donna, and perhaps Susan (still a preschooler) could come home after that. We would bring Anita home when the doctor and Ray and I determined that I would be able to care for her.

Our plan went reasonably well — at first. We did bring Ken and Donna home, but in a couple of weeks I felt exhausted again. Rest didn't bring relief. Part of the problem was that the medicine I was taking had lost its effect, so my doctor had increased my dosage. That helped me in some ways, but I started getting more headaches, and that made my fear grow. I made breakfast and lunch for the children, but relatives and friends took care of them when they were done with school for the day. The seemingly simple task of making dinner became very difficult for me. It took me all day to plan and prepare the food. Peeling potatoes or even breaking lettuce for salad took hours. I mocked myself for wanting to do more than "homemaking."

Trying to control my thoughts rather than allowing them to control me was wearing me out; often I failed at the attempt. My doctor didn't have to tell me that "forgetting is almost impossible." I was experiencing that fact. Substitute, substitute, he had said, but my determination and my energy began to fail, and I stopped trying.

Even my outpatient therapy sessions didn't lift my increasing depression. After my third session, my doctor made these notes:

She is beginning to show more of her true self and her depressive mood than she has for some months.

The problems which she faces are exactly the same as those which she had when she was in the hospital, but perhaps due to the excitement and newness of the situation in going home, they have not been very well expressed during the last two visits. There continues to remain the problem of what she should do in the Kingdom in addition to her family responsibilities as regards her children and husband. She continually feels that there must be more that needs to be done and that she should contribute more of her time and use it more advantageously. [A devilish joke! I couldn't even care for my family.]

She constantly struggles with the idea that she has so many material things and that things are easy for her because of modern [housekeeping] conveniences, and that this extra time should be employed in a special way for some special purpose. She also struggles with the problem of whether to write or not. She feels that if she writes she will be writing for publication, and, although at this time she denies it, the [issue] probably is the same as it was before, which is that if she writes she will be writing for her own self-aggrandizement, and with the idea of seeing the material which she constructed — in print. Along this same line, anything which gives her particular satisfaction she feels is wrong and she is not entitled to it.

This woman continues to be depressed but she is now once again beginning to bring forward the items which cause her distress. . . . She continues to have one of the children home, but not always the same one. On occasion there are two of them at a time. She finds that having two at a time upsets her. She realizes but finds it very difficult to accept the fact that she cannot do things outside of her responsibility to her own family, when she does not even have her own family all together under one roof.

Besides this she gives a typical history of migraine attacks of which she has had two in the last three weeks. She awakens with them in the morning; sometimes they awaken her. There is a feeling of a burning sensation around and in the eyes, accompanied by a feeling of nausea and inability to take food. They last from twenty-four to forty-eight, or sometimes seventy-two hours. She is given [medicine] and a return appointment in two weeks.

After this session I was still depressed, but I left my doctor's office with new determination. I would lick this thing yet. Maybe I wasn't sick after all; maybe I just had to act as though it was all in my head, as so many people say, and go on with my life. A plan was forming in my mind that had to do with an appealing ad I had seen in the newspaper just a few days earlier.

My sister-in-law had driven me to the doctor's office. (I hadn't driven since before Ray and I had left the States for Africa because I was too afraid to do it.) She and I talked a bit about my therapy, but I didn't tell her about my plan.

Maybe it would be the answer to my problems.

Just for Credit

The words of the wise are like goads . . .
given by one Shepherd. . . .
Of making many books there is no end,
and much study wearies the body.

Ecclesiastes 12:11-12

ALTHOUGH I hadn't told Ray, I had saved a newspaper ad for the local junior college. I had made up my mind: I would enroll there to see if I could handle a course at the college level. No, the kindly voice answered when I called, it's not too late to enroll for the fall semester.

After I had completed my enrollment and purchased books, I told Ray that I intended to take an introductory course in literature. The class was held at night, when he could care for the children. Maybe going to school would help me get my mind off myself. So far, in spite of my will, I hadn't been too successful at that, but I kept on trying. I knew that recovery was up to me. Yes, I had enrolled for credit. Why not? Did it make any difference? I didn't think so. Ray reluctantly agreed it might be worth a try, although he expressed doubt about my timing. Wasn't it a bit too soon?

My first class was on a Tuesday in September. I spent all day washing windows, although I didn't finish the job. I had no energy and moved slowly. My arms ached with the up-and-down efforts I was making. I persisted doggedly, even though I took no pride in the work. Tomorrow it would rain anyway, I thought. Still, my plan for the evening made the work a little easier.

The rain wasn't kind enough to wait until Wednesday. It began as I waited for the bus early that evening. An omen? I was afraid. Only Ray knew of my plan; I hadn't told anyone else, not my mother especially. It had been two weeks since I had enrolled and had bought my books. Ray and I couldn't really afford the cost of tuition and books, but . . . I would get a college education, no matter how long it would take. This was something I had desired since I was a little girl. I would be able to read good literature and understand it. I would learn about the great religions of the world. I would study history and discover what made our country what it is. Nothing would stop me.

My head pounded, and I felt a little sick to my stomach. Never mind, I told myself. Go anyway. You have to take the initiative if you're ever going to get over this stupid illness. I was shaking.

I had almost turned back when the bus pulled up at the corner. I got on, glancing at the other passengers. Good — nobody I knew. No one even looked at me. The pounding in my head kept rhythm with the beating of my heart.

The driver had gone only a few blocks when my stomach turned upside down. With great difficulty I pulled the rope for the exit bell, got off when the driver stopped, and managed not to throw up until I stepped down to the sidewalk. By this time the rain was coming down steadily.

I was in a residential area near home, and I sat on the lawn, clutching my head, my purse, and my new books. I apologized to God for attempting to do what he obviously didn't want me to do.

Even though it was pouring, I shuffled home. I needed a little time before I could face Ray. When I got back to the house, he was surprised to see me. "What happened?" he asked.

When I told him, he felt sorry that it hadn't worked out. "Maybe you shouldn't think about it just now," he said. "You have plenty of time; maybe you can try later."

But at that point I abandoned all hope of going to college.

Since I had enrolled in the class without consulting my doctor, I felt very disobedient. I had violated authority, and my conscience accused me harshly. I hated the prospect of telling my doctor, but I would.

I didn't get much sleep that night. My headache developed into a full migraine that lasted several days. When I felt a little better, I called my doctor and asked to see him as soon as possible. I remembered the words of the Preacher: "much study wearies the body." How much would God have to discipline me before I realized that college was not in his plan for me?

When I met with my doctor and told him what I had done, I felt like a naughty child. For a moment he said nothing, and neither did I. A mixture of defiance and fear engulfed me.

"You enrolled for credit?" he asked.

"Yes."

"Why?"

I didn't answer.

We began to talk about education. "Do you think college is an automatic road to knowledge?" he asked. No, I didn't believe that, but I thought that a college degree represented the acquisition of various kinds of knowledge and that it gave a person the tools to keep learning. Besides, it seemed to me that the common perception was that college graduates had something that society needed. Somehow people with a college *degree* had a key to many doors that were locked for people who didn't have one. I felt like an amateur when I wanted to be a professional.

I wanted to do more than read the Bible — I wanted to study textbooks. And I wanted to be a teacher — that had been my dream for as long as I could remember. Reading had been and still was (if I could learn to concentrate again) my favorite pastime, and I was a quick learner. Why shouldn't I go to college? My head pounded.

When I was in grade school and junior high, several of my teachers had told my parents that I had "college potential." But these assessments had never moved Ma. I remembered how traumatic it had been for me when my parents had told me they couldn't send me to college. Ma strongly believed that girls didn't need to go to college — they only got married anyway, she said (which I did, one year after high school). I talked with Pa separately. He wasn't as convinced as Ma that it was pointless for a girl to go to college, but he explained that it was also a matter of money. We were in the middle of the Depression, and he couldn't afford to send all his children to college, so he would have to send the boys. I promised that I would pay my own way, even though I didn't have the foggiest notion where I would get the money.

To my surprise, my parents allowed me to enroll in what was called the "college preparatory" program when I first went to high school. I worked about fifteen hours a week in a bakery, and my earnings paid my tuition for the program. I studied hard — Latin, geometry, and more. I loved it, and I did well.

But when I was about halfway through the tenth grade,

my parents told me I would have to change my college-preparatory track to a business track. They told me that they couldn't afford to let me save money for college even if I earned it myself, because they needed my earnings to help with family expenses if the boys were going to be able to use their earnings for college. I pleaded with my parents to change their minds about this, and I talked to Pa about it often, because he at least understood my ambition. To strengthen her argument that I shouldn't go to college, Ma said that my government teacher had told Pa and her that I wasn't as bright as my older brother but that I got top grades by working hard. That was probably true, I said, but should that keep me from going to college? I got excellent grades, didn't I? My teacher's remark showed that I was trying hard, didn't it?

I accused my parents of favoring my brothers, which they denied. It was a matter of being practical, they said. I became angry, rude, and insolent whenever we discussed this. I was angry at my mother for convincing my father to agree with her. I was angry at my father for supporting her decision. Ma repeated again and again her litany about girls' roles. Pa begged me to try to understand. "Ma always tells me that no one will want to marry me," I cried, "so why isn't education just as important for me?" They didn't hear me. "You're wrong, wrong, wrong!" I would shout; then I would leave the room to cry alone.

I was very disappointed with my parents' decision, but I did as I was told. When I graduated from high school, I became a legal secretary and bookkeeper. Even though this wasn't the job of my dreams, I did enjoy the work. Half of my wages and half of any raise I got went to my parents — while my older brother could save his money for school. Often I was jealous.

At this point in my story, my doctor said, "It seems to me that you're more interested in the *degree* than in the education itself."

His comment was like a knife twisting in my heart. Was he right? Was that what I wanted? I had learned to be fiercely honest with him. I looked at him, then looked down at my hands as I twisted the tissue I held. My tears flowed freely. I thought of my desire to do more than care for my family — and now my inability to take care of my children and my home, let alone go to college. Caring for my family was an enormous task that I still wasn't accomplishing. Ray and I still had only Ken and Donna at home, and only part-time. I must have been crazy to think I could go to college. Maybe my parents had been right all along. Why couldn't I just be satisfied with reading the literature books I had bought? But still, if that's all there was to college, why didn't everybody just read the books? I felt confused and defeated. My desire to learn more and my determination to be content with the plenty that I had were like oil and water — they just didn't mix.

Long, silent minutes passed. When the telephone rang, my doctor let it ring. He handed me another tissue and waited.

I looked up. I knew he would wait for me to say something.

"That's not true," I blurted, finally responding to his observation.

"Then why did you sign up for credit? Why didn't you just audit the classes — at least until you could see how it would go?" He asked this gently, but this was the closest he ever came to scolding me. I regretted what I had done.

I had no answer to his question, but I still believed he wasn't completely right. Still, the evidence seemed to support his opinion, not mine. I wanted an education badly, but yes, I did want credit too. Was that so wrong?

After some discussion, I had to agree with my doctor that while it might not be permanently unfeasible for me to continue my education, now was not the time for me to become entangled with the demands of college courses. He said that if I really wanted an *education,* he would recommend that for now I read some books that would go a long way to prepare me for college, should that opportunity present itself one day. Why not? I thought. I would never get better; I felt certain of that again.

He recommended a set of fifty books, *The Harvard Classics,* and pointed out that sometimes used sets could be gotten very inexpensively. Ray and I watched the classified ads every day and found a set for twenty-five dollars. At first I had trouble concentrating. It took quite a while before I could read many of the books in the set, especially the difficult ones, but during the next several years, I read these classics from cover to cover.

Meanwhile, life was again becoming more difficult for me. As my depression increased, I felt like the mountain I had to climb every day became higher. But I kept struggling. I wouldn't go back to that hospital again — not if I could help it.

Again

Be merciful to me, O Lord, for I {again}
am in distress . . .
my strength fails because of my affliction,
and my bones grow weak.

Psalm 31:9-10

BOTH Ken and Donna were in school part of the day, and because they spent much of the rest of the day with relatives nearby, I had hoped I would find time for activities besides homemaking. Since I had cut short my experiment with college, that didn't require my time. Still, I was always "busy" with housework, mainly because I put so much time and effort into each task I undertook.

I was again working hard at substituting positive thoughts for negative ones, but it was a challenge. Negative thoughts bobbed to the surface of my mind repeatedly. My illness rose and fell like ocean waves, picking me up and pulling me down with it. I could feel myself being lifted up, up, up. Then suddenly the peace would crest, and depression would pull me underwater. I couldn't tell exactly what — what thoughts, what events — caused my frequent drownings.

As hard as I worked at "thinking good thoughts," I worked harder at trying to keep house, cook and bake, keep up with the laundry, and sew for the children. I deliberately attacked my perfectionism, avoiding doing anything perfectly. I felt awful: my head pounded and my stomach knotted. Being a wife and mother took all of my time. I had been a fool to think I had time for any activities outside the family — yet I couldn't stop longing for them. God, would I never learn the secret of contentment?

As September wore on, I wore down. Depression sucked me downward into another vortex of despair. Merely being alive was war. What had happened to that will to live victoriously which I had claimed just a couple of months ago? The vicious cycle had started again. Would I never be well? Would I always be a cross for my husband to bear? My guilt increased.

In late September 1954, Ken and Donna were again sent to relatives and I went back into the hospital. My doctor made these notes about my readmission:

> During the last several contacts with this woman as an out-patient, she has had a very drawn and worried expression on her face. It is quite evident that she is still depressive in her mood. There is definite improvement as far as her progress in adjusting to her mother is concerned and also she is beginning to gain the idea that her first task is to give of herself to her family and not feel constantly that she must do some writing or other kingdom work. This has been difficult for her to see because while she realizes that the children need her attention she has constantly been of the opinion that ways and means can be found for doing the housework more efficiently, leaving time for writing. . . .

The factor of her ability to accomplish her housework — probably due to the fact that she is driven by forces within her — gives rise to the good report as given by the patient and her husband. [This does] not match the situation as it is encountered in the office during her interviews. . . . The forces within her which drive her continue to permit her to take care of the house but it is quite obvious that the depression itself is deepening. She states that she has no more antagonism towards her mother and believes this difficulty to be solved. She also, for the first time, states that she now realizes that she cannot take care of the children and do writing and speaking and attend meetings. . . . She has given up the idea of doing these extra things but presents them in an attitude of defeat saying it was . . . foolish [for her to try to do them].

The patient cries very easily. I believe[d] that she should come in and yesterday I telephoned her husband to check up on her activities, etc. The suggestion that she return to the hospital [came] as a surprise, but the patient herself has frequently mentioned during the last few weeks that she knows something is happening within her. . . . Her husband says she is constantly on the move, seeming to find something to do all the time, being uneasy unless she thinks of something to be done. It seems that she cannot rest but is driven. . . .

She is always tense. She again feels self-accusative but this time it is not on a special point but in general [she] feels useless and worthless. In contrast to some previous visits she is more hopeless [about the possibility of] recovery. . . . The constant driving anxiety [about] activity is retarding her progress.

While I was hospitalized, I received several shock treatments. They confused my thoughts; I couldn't deal with my problems logically. I complained to my doctor that the treatments didn't help me remember the good parts of my life and didn't help me forget the bad. Here I was, hospitalized again. I believed that I had already exposed myself to the core, but I still wasn't able to practice the skills I needed to regain my mental health. If God wanted something of me, why didn't he at least let me know what it was?

Earlier I had told my doctor that I had reconciled myself to my mother. I had made a beginning by refusing to allow her to control me. But now, since my depression had returned, I wondered if I was still really angry. Had I forgiven my mother only with my thoughts and words and not with my feelings? I complained to my doctor that he didn't help me with my feelings.

In response to my complaint, he and I discussed anger during the next two sessions I had with him. The things he taught me about anger were things I had never learned at home, in school, or in church.

Anger results from pain, frustration, or fear. It is a natural, healthy response, but many Christians are convinced, wrongly, that anger is sin. (That's what I believed at the time.) We try to check it or repress it. We fail to examine what caused it. We even deny that we've experienced it. Or if we recognize that we're angry, we feel guilty. I thought I had faced and accepted my anger, but it seemed to have done little good.

My doctor helped me to see that Ma's anger and frustration with me may have had its roots in fear. She knew the role I would have to fill as an adult female, and she felt obligated to train me for it. So, when I resisted her training, it frightened her, and she expressed her fear by getting angry with me. Her methods of dealing with me had been unfair and unjust, even cruel, and they had made me angry. But as a child I had been unable to handle my anger properly.

People's sensitivity to anger varies. A harsh word, even quietly spoken, crushes one person, while a pain-inflicting slap doesn't daunt another. How long anger lasts also varies from person to person. One of our daughters, a very amateur pianist, used to use the keyboard to vent her frustration and anger. Playing a page or two of hymns or marching music on either all black or all white keys produced a cacophony that erased her anger. Moments later — thank goodness — her recital was over and her anger was gone.

As a child, I was angry often, but I didn't have such a healthy way of venting my feelings. Since I believed that anger was sin, I tried to suppress it. When Ma and I did have an argument, I knew that I would have to face her as well as God. After my initial outburst, I would say little. I would smother the anger and ponder the incident and the pain for several days. Sometimes I would pout, which only prolonged Ma's anger. The sad thing was that we fed each other's anger and frustration.

By the time I was a teenager, I paid a high price when I did vent my anger. My windpipe would constrict, the veins above my ears would bulge, and my eyes would burn as I tried to hold back tears. My stomach would get queasy, seeming to twist from side to side. My knees would feel like two small balloons that would deflate if I moved. After any such expression of anger — especially toward Ma — I would invariably get a migraine headache.

There are biological reasons to explain why I would feel so bad. Anger increases adrenaline production, which in turn increases blood circulation in the brain. This causes the brain to swell, and since it is encased in the rigid, unyielding skull, the internal pressure causes the pain of the headache. And certain kinds of people are particularly likely to get these headaches, as O. Quentin Hyder explains in *The Christian's Handbook of Psychiatry*: "Migraine headaches . . . usually occur in high-strung, ambitious, perfectionistic, driving personalities who are products of rigid conventional families who have high standards and demanding, unforgiving expectations of all members."

The fallout of repressed or unrecognized anger hurts not only the angry person but also those who may be convenient targets for the angry person to lash out against. In fact, someone who represses anger frequently takes it out on someone other than the person who brought on the anger. Had I perhaps been the scapegoat for much of Ma's unresolved anger against someone else? Could she have been angry about the ways in which society limited her role as a woman? I don't know. What I do know is that when I was a child I felt that I *myself* was the disappointment that incurred her wrath. I hadn't learned how to discern that she was angry and frustrated with my behavior, not with my actual self.

Little did I realize that my unhealthy capacity to bury anger provided both the seed and the soil for my present illness. Unresolved anger is devilish, malicious, lonely, painful; so is depression. As a child I didn't know that; I knew only that anger was sin. Now I was learning not only the difference between good and bad anger, righteous and unrighteous anger, but also the need to deal with its causes. When its presence is denied, its evil is multiplied. It becomes emotional cancer. That's why anger must be recognized, acknowledged, and exposed, especially when it is turned on one's self and it rots into guilt. I had been guilty and ashamed of being angry, and now I was reaping that bitter harvest.

How Long?

SOMEONE HAS SAID that "depression is anger turned inward." This, at least in part, applied to me. Often, my doctor said, the person who suffers from depression needs help in discovering its sources, and I was thankful he was helping me. I would never have conceded that the roots of my depression and anger reached back to my childhood if I had been able to hobble along in life without being hospitalized. A lifetime will not be long enough for me to live my gratitude for the benefits God gave me through my illness. But I didn't see it this way at first. I hadn't wanted to admit that I was ill with depression, and being hospitalized certainly didn't seem like a blessing.

That was actually part of God's intervention and wisdom, but that became apparent to me only over time.

Again my minister helped me. I told him that I had been sick long enough, that God probably did make lots of people well, but not me. Why? Hadn't I been trying my best? Except for my stupid attempt to go to college, I had followed my doctor's prescriptions well: taking the children back one at a time, walking frequently, resting regularly, listening to music, talking with more people, substituting positive thoughts for negative ones. What more did God want? What was God trying to prove? I wasn't better. I had admitted my faults and short-comings, hadn't I? I had accepted forgiveness (graciously, I thought); I was free, liberated. Still, I *felt* rotten. Why not close the door, forget the past, and start a new life?

"I'm not sure that you would want to forget the past completely," my pastor said. "If you could forget, how would you ever build on it? The work comes in pruning and shaping those traits and characteristics that you now have recognized as less than you want them to be. And of course God will help you."

I wasn't so sure. It seemed to me that if God was paying attention to me, I wouldn't be in the hospital again.

My minister took out his Bible and asked me to take out mine. We read Psalm 77 together again, as we had some months before. I felt that the psalmist and I were kindred spirits. My pastor called my attention to a few verses in particular:

> I cried out to God for help;
> I cried out to God to hear me.
> When I was in distress, I sought the Lord;
> at night I stretched out untiring hands
> and my soul refused to be comforted.
> I remembered you, O God, and I groaned . . .
> I was too troubled to speak. . . .

150

Will [God] never show his favor again?
Has his unfailing love vanished forever?
Has God forgotten to be merciful?
Has he in anger withheld his compassion?

(vv. 1-4, 7-8)

I interrupted our reading. Was the psalmist depressed too? Why did God let his people suffer so much and so long? My faith was sustaining me only very weakly at this point, and my doubts troubled me, so I was heartened to see that even a strong believer like the psalmist questioned what God was permitting to happen to him.

My minister continued to read:

Your ways, O God, are holy.
What god is so great as our God? . . .
Your path led through the sea,
your way through the mighty waters,
though your footprints were not seen.

(vv. 13, 19)

He reminded me that God always remembers. He never lets go of his own. But he does not always reveal why he has chosen a particular path for us — we do not always see his footprints. My minister showed me that if I believed — and I did — that God was not withholding his compassion from me *in anger*, then I could also believe the rest of the psalm. He *would* lead me on the path he had already prepared for my life.

God's words, through my minister, renewed my hope.

Further therapy sessions with my doctor also strengthened me both physically and emotionally, and after two months, in mid-November, I was allowed to return home — although my doctor discharged me reluctantly, and stipulated that the children couldn't be at home with me right away. He recorded this comment about my discharge:

> She was discharged somewhat prematurely because of the excessive homesickness and insistence on going home which she displayed. The situation at home was such that the conditions were considered to be favorable enough for her to try it at home. This, in connection with the factor of [her] having been a patient here before, and the understanding which her husband has, made the trial at home seem reasonable.

It was a challenge to be out of the hospital again. Part of the problem was that my doctor had changed my medication, and I felt dull as a consequence. Two weeks later, Ken and Donna returned home, but I had little energy. Often I went back to bed after they had left for school. I was frequently immobilized by anxiety. I needed help, but having someone around made it worse. Some of my fear I kept from Ray because I was afraid that if I told him about it, he would tell my doctor, and then I would have to go back to the hospital. I felt better in the evening when he came home from work.

I was willing now to settle for becoming *any kind* of person. Even just enough of one to function as a wife and mother.

This thought surprised me. It was the first time I had consciously and spontaneously *wanted* to be "just" a wife and mother. To my joy, I also realized that this desire wasn't new; I had always had it. I had always loved — and enjoyed — my husband, my children, and my home. Having children so close to each other in age had made me very busy, but never had I wished my situation was different. A burden rolled away as I realized that my guilt feelings about my role as wife and mother were part of my illness.

With my minister's help, I also realized that I didn't have

to feel guilty about not "doing" more. To *be* a Christian, my minister said, is just that — *being*; too often we think it is *doing.* The doing will follow, he said, out of gratitude to God, but being a child of God is what's most important. My misperception of kingdom work was also part of my illness, I realized.

Although I had cooperated with my doctor throughout my illness, I had not until now disentangled myself completely from the idea that I was sinning rather than showing signs of sickness. Now I recognized that depression is a disease, the virus of distress at its deepest personal level. I told Ray that I was totally committed to doing whatever was necessary to get well as fast as possible — even if it meant returning to the hospital. At this point, I was still having some difficulty. My anxiety hadn't lessened, and my uncontrollable drive still pushed me. I cried daily and often.

I continued to see my doctor once or twice a week, and he and I discussed my efforts to overcome my passion for perfection. He made these notes on the subject:

> This woman has not been enjoying her housework. It develops in consultation today that she has been so hateful toward herself for an element of perfectionism in her that she has been deliberately avoiding any trace of it in the work which she does around the house. The result has been that she has had no satisfaction whatever in doing housework and it has become a drudgery. Formerly it was a pleasure. This matter is gone into and she is told that she should indulge in some of these perfectionist feelings if that is what they should be called and also that a certain element of perfectionism is necessary in any kind of work in order to do a good job of it. . . .
>
> I feel that this woman needs to resume her work in [the] manner in which she always did it and thereby find satisfaction [in] it.

Somewhere in my train of twisted thought I had acquired the idea that if Christians really like what they're doing, then they're doing it for themselves, and if they're doing it for themselves — and not a hundred percent for God — then their work is faulty, defiled. This idea fit the either-or pattern of my life. I remembered one of the teachings of the Heidelberg Catechism, a doctrinal statement of the denomination to which I belong: "Even our best works in this life are all imperfect and defiled with sin." I had learned in my youth that even our best deeds are like "filthy rags."

My doctor now explained that I misunderstood this idea completely. Doing something well — whether it's housework, ministering, teaching, or something else — does please God, but he doesn't expect us not to take pleasure in our tasks. He gives us different gifts, and he expects us to develop them and use them with joy and delight. And up until now I had been fixated on the idea that enjoying one's gifts defiled them. Because of my misguided idea, I had purposely tried not to enjoy my housework, which for me meant not doing it particularly well. I had been skipping routine dusting, overlooking corners, and hardly folding laundry to prove to God that I was doing these things for him and not for myself. I had been controlled by my childhood concept of working as the road to acceptance. But after talking with my doctor I realized that I had been unfairly robbing myself of satisfaction in my work. With this new idea in place, I gradually began to take pleasure in keeping my home clean, neat, and nicely decorated.

The doctor commented on my progress:

> Today she says that keeping house has again become somewhat of a pleasure for her insofar as she can enjoy anything.
>
> She still has trouble going out into groups. She has

been invited to attend society meetings but finds that she doesn't feel that she can do so. It is remarked to her that it is quite obvious that a thinking individual would be ill at ease going to meetings and attending various social affairs when she is not yet doing the primary business of her life which is that of caring for her family. She recognizes this factor and seems relieved when once again told that her hesitancy in going out to public places will be very likely present until she is caring for her whole family.

In early December of 1954, our third child, Susan, returned to the family. The children, young as they were, helped me. They "made" their beds, picked up their clothes when I asked them to, ran little errands, and did other small tasks. I was pleased, but I longed for the day when our baby would be able to come home too.

Early in 1955, I was once again sucked under by a wave of depression. Our three children were sent to stay with relatives for a week, but I managed to stay out of the hospital. It was now fifteen months since Ray and I had returned to the States. My doctor told me that I would probably continue to experience such episodes for some time, and in some ways this helped me to cope, knowing that it was "normal" for me to have these bouts of depression.

But wouldn't they ever stop?

Respite

The Lord revives my failing strength,
he makes my joy complete;
and in right paths, for his name's sake,
he guides my faltering feet.

"The Lord, My Shepherd,
Rules My Life," stanza 2*

MY PROGRESS was extremely slow, but real. When I looked back eighteen months, or even twelve months, I could see that my life now was more manageable. I had some control. I had hope — shaky, but genuine. But I found myself newly troubled by the notion that I was remiss because I wasn't directly involved in "kingdom work." If God wanted me to be busy in his work, why didn't he give me strength for it?

I was also affected by the fact that now Ray occasionally

mentioned returning to the mission field. Thinking about Africa hurt me; I became depressed and cried often. I was haunted by the idea that I was self-centered and selfish. Eventually Ray called my doctor to ask about the possibility of our returning to Africa. The doctor made these comments in my file:

> Her husband asks regarding the future of doing missionary work as he wishes to write a letter to the Board of Missions which is [having] its annual meeting at this time. He wonders whether he should mention that if there should be an opening for construction work in the future on the mission field, he would like to be considered. He is advised against this and advised merely to mention that he continues to have a strong interest in mission work and continues to support it by his prayers and other methods in whatever field missionary efforts may be carried on. He likes this idea and agrees to it. I did not know until the conversation with him today that there was such a strong desire within the husband to return to the foreign field of missions. He does not talk about it [to anyone] as he knows it is impossible to do anyway.

Returning to Nigeria, then, was out of the question.

On the home front, I was trying to expand my little circle of activity. My first venture into what was then a woman's world was attending a parent-teachers' meeting at the children's school. I was composed outside but shaky inside. I responded briefly to greetings, but I left the meeting before it was over because I was afraid I might get involved in a conversation, and that prospect still bothered me.

These women seemed so ambitious, so active, so self-confident. They had so many plans. I was staggered by their ideas and their goals, and I went home crying. I couldn't be part of anything like that yet, I decided; first I had to concentrate on my family and get all four of the children home. It took a week for me to regain my composure. It took eighteen months for me to feel comfortable enough to attend another group activity.

When I had my next appointment with my doctor, I asked him where these women found the time to accomplish so much. "God gives every person twenty-four hours a day," he said, "and each of us decides how to use that time. Some women have less work than others; others have more energy. Some have one ambition; others have a variety of interests they pursue." It seemed to me that I didn't have any choices; they had been made for me.

And right now having a family was a full-time job for me.

Again I started thinking about having Ken, Donna, and Susie home permanently, not staying with relatives three or four days a week. But, more than that, I was thinking of getting baby Anita home. It scared me, but I felt an urgent impulse to do it. I thought I was doing reasonably well — but was I doing well enough? I was still on medication, and it disappointed me that I still tired so easily and needed so much rest. I didn't see how routine housework could wear me out. And Anita wasn't even home yet!

My worries about being a good mother to Anita deepened. The friends who were taking care of her were very attached to her, and she was very attached to them; right now they were her family. That was a painful thing for Ray and me to acknowledge. Even so, Ray accepted this as the normal course of events under the circumstances, which it was. I understood it too, I guess, with my head, but it was very hard for me to accept emotionally.

My doctor and I discussed my relationship with Anita. I vowed I would never make the mistakes my mother had. If she or any of our other children would show any sign of emotional disturbance, Ray and I would seek the help of a Christian psychologist or psychiatrist immediately. Despite my determination to do everything right, I did make mistakes — many mistakes. A mother's illness does affect her family, I was to find out.

Meanwhile, I continued to improve. I was comforted by something God had said through the prophet Jeremiah, a verse my minister had called to my attention: "'For I know the plans I have for you,' declares the Lord, 'plans to prosper you and not to harm you, plans to give you hope and a future'" (29:11).

Over time I had fewer and fewer sessions with my doctor. At first the time between sessions lengthened to two weeks, then to a month, then even to six weeks. Eventually my doctor said I could call when I felt I needed an appointment. At this juncture in my treatment he wrote, "The final diagnosis . . . is actually Manic Depressive Psychosis, but within this there is a great deal of psychoneurotic element characterized by anxiety, fear, and a definite paranoid element."

I was not yet completely well. Peace was still elusive for me. And I still struggled with my inability to find time or energy to do what I had mistakenly labeled "kingdom work." But I had worked hard and prayed much about that problem. And I had forgiven my mother. What possibly could remain of my faulty thinking and repressed anger?

True, my mother and I did not have the kind of open mother-daughter relationship that she would have liked. And I still disappointed her. But I thought that I was mature enough to be able to live with my present understanding of the situation and accept the fact that I, not she, would have to change.

I was wrong. My broken-record syndrome recurred — during the day and even at night when my head kept me from sleeping.

It wasn't over yet.

Truth and Its Perception

{Your beauty} should be that of your inner self,
the unfading beauty of a gentle and quiet spirit,
which is of great worth in God's sight.

1 Peter 3:4

THAT I WAS STILL emotionally weak became clear to me the next autumn. In July 1955 my parents went to the Netherlands for three months. While they were gone, I began to feel alive. I felt better than I had during any time since my illness had begun in early 1953, before Anita's birth. I still communicated with them, writing them every week or so about the children and the church.

Three weeks before they were scheduled to come back to the States, I received a letter from Ma in which she commented that I really hadn't written her as much as she would have liked. She suggested that I write immediately and send my letter airmail, so she would receive one more letter before they returned. I wondered if she had written my brothers a similar letter.

I wrote, of course. At great cost. I spent the next two weeks on a slow-moving roller coaster, headed downward. When a couple of my brothers and I greeted my parents at the train station, I felt awful: my head seemed like it was going to burst, and my stomach flip-flopped. I had feared going to the station, but I had been even more afraid of the consequences of not going. We took Ma and Pa home, but my head ached and I felt sick to my stomach, so I stayed only a little while. Ma frowned when I left but said nothing. But when I didn't attend the family gathering a few days later, Ma was very angry.

I made an appointment with my doctor at Pine Rest and shared with him my disappointment in myself. Why had I reacted so dramatically to seeing Ma again? If I had forgiven Ma — and I had — why did I become physically ill when I was with her? Why did I feel guilty? We talked a long time, and he quieted my anxiety. He made these notes on our session:

There is no doubt about it that there is difficulty between these two. They do not seem to see eye to eye on anything. The patient expresses it not as any hatred for her mother but rather an intolerance for her. She has a great deal of guilt about this because she states that she has no right to feel the way that she does when her mother has been so good to her. On the other hand she points out that all of her four brothers seem to feel the same way toward their mother. It is pointed out to her that [her emotional difficulties do not spring from] the fact that she feels as she does toward her mother since she does this on a purely logical level and realizes that she has reason to feel the way she does — and I believe she does to some extent — but . . . rather the way that she accepts this fact of being antagonistic toward her mother rather than loving and showing a high degree of daughterly concern. It is recalled to my mind that at the very beginning the father pointed out that the mother was a difficult person and that statement is on the front page of her (Lillian's) history.

. . . The general picture here is one of guilt regarding her mother, and this is a prominent one. The historical picture is such that the interviews in the future should take into consideration the factor of her mother's place in the patient's life.

Again my doctor showed me that just because I had forgiven Ma, that didn't automatically erase the many hurts in my history with her.

How difficult it is to forgive. Forgiveness is a process, a Christian art that I hadn't learned too well at that point. The book by Lewis Smedes entitled *Forgive and Forget: Healing the Hurts We Don't Deserve,* published in the mid-eighties, would have been a big help to me at that time. This passage in particular would have given me an important insight:

> Is there anger after forgiving?
> Yes, often. It can't be helped.
> Some people believe that they should not feel anger in their hearts once they forgive.
> I do not agree. I think that anger and forgiving can live together in the same heart. You are not a failure at forgiving just because you are still angry that a painful wrong was done to you. It is terribly unrealistic to expect a single act of forgiving to get rid of all angry feelings.
> . . . You cannot erase the past, you can only heal the pain it has left behind.

My doctor basically made this point in his counseling with me. "The wounds you have are deep," he pointed out. "You'll probably be affected by them as long as you live. Your mother will control you as long as you permit her to do so. She's a constant in your life that you have to learn to deal with. It's something like people who live in a flood area; the floods come again and again. How do people cope with that?"

My doctor changed my prescription somewhat, but that didn't help me much. I felt drugged and dopey during the day, yet not rested or relaxed. I would go to bed after supper, unable to sleep, then sleep a couple of hours, and then lie awake — endlessly — until morning.

This went on for two weeks. I hung on. I hated to call my doctor because I feared being hospitalized again. Maybe I would just be an emotional wreck for the rest of my life. Maybe the children would be sent away again. It didn't seem fair of God to make my children and my husband suffer this way. After all, I was the one who messed things up.

One morning, after Ray had left for work and the children had left for school, I became hysterical. Not knowing what else to do, I called my doctor. He made this note about our conversation:

> This morning she is in a panic. She does not know what to do with herself. She has tried to call her husband and cannot get hold of him. She thought of calling her father, but then she will have to tell him how she feels towards her mother, and she thinks that this would hurt her father very much. The fact of the matter is that the father recognizes that there is a difficulty between the two on the part of their feelings toward each other although there are no actual outward words or bickering between them.

I hung on a bit longer, but two weeks later I was admitted to Pine Rest for the third time. It was early November. The children were sent to stay with relatives. I was in that devilish, lonely pit again. Once again I was given a series of shock treatments, and I dreaded them as much as I had before.

I began to fear that it would be a long time before the family would be together again. I wondered how long my husband would be able to live with five children instead of four children and a wife. But Ray was unwavering in his support of me.

My father often dropped in to say hello in the afternoon, and shortly before my return to the hospital, I confided in him a bit. "I don't want to be like Ma," I said, "and run the lives of the whole family. Why doesn't she leave me alone?"

"*Ja,* I know, Lily," said Pa, "she is that way, but she doesn't mean it that way. She feels bad that you are sick." After our visit, Pa, at my doctor's request, went to his office. Pa explained to my doctor that I interpreted Ma's suggestions as commands indicating that she felt that I was unable to run my own home without her help. When my doctor told me this, I laughed bitterly. "I guess she's right, isn't she? I can't even stay out of the hospital!"

Pa also told my doctor that Ma had many good qualities that I was unable to see. I didn't think that was true; I tried to see her good traits, and I did see some. But it seemed to me that when he or Ray said "You're just like Ma," they weren't referring to her good points. I knew that Pa thought I had some of her "good qualities," but what he didn't know was that I wanted no part of them! Yet, I accused myself, I did accept *things* from her. Ma and I had never been able to communicate well, but since Ray and I had come back from Nigeria, she had given me a delicate china breakfast set that she had received as a wedding present. It was precious to her, and it was her way of saying, "I care," but I was too miserable to hear her.

At this point my doctor wanted to see Ma. After talking with her, he concluded that she had only my welfare at heart.

Of course, I thought, but he had never walked in my shoes. Why was it so hard for me to believe that my mother's intentions were good? Shouldn't a Christian daughter believe her Christian mother? For a while after this my doctor and I got no further in my therapy; my needle was stuck in the groove of guilt — again.

In time my guilt feelings eased. I longed to *feel* warm and loving toward Ma, and I discussed this with my minister. He helped me to think differently about love. "Love, genuine love," he said, "is not necessarily a *feeling*. How many times have you read in Scripture that Christ *felt* love for people?" I thought of John, the disciple Jesus loved. I thought of Mary and Martha and his love for them.

"Just because you don't read that Jesus *felt* love doesn't mean that he didn't love, does it?" he asked. Of course not, I realized. My minister explained that in Jesus Christ, love is doing. "If you love me," we read in John 14:15, "you will obey what I command."

"Even the second commandment begins with *do* and not with *feel*," my minister continued. "*Do* unto others as you would have them do unto you. That's love." He explained that the fifth commandment doesn't mean that we are to remain under our parents' control. The greatest honor a child can give her parents is to be independent, to be able to stand on her own two feet, to separate herself from them and give herself wholly to her husband and children. "Yes, sometimes the *feeling* of love follows," my minister concluded, "but that isn't necessary. Jesus *did* the supreme act of love: he died for us."

It was so simple. Why hadn't I understood the *doing* aspect of love before? Up until now, *doing* had had only legalistic, self-righteous connotations for me. Suddenly my thoughts turned not to Jesus, not to my mother, but to my husband, who had *done* so much for me. I began to cry. My minister touched my arm and stayed with me until I had regained my composure.

In another few weeks, after I had received a few more shock treatments, I felt calm enough to have another session with my doctor. He noticed a difference in me, which he commented on in his record of my treatment:

> The patient looks a great deal better than when she was seen last time. She says she has felt almost her normal self this past week. This is the first time she has felt this way since she came into the hospital. She is beginning to see some of the ramifications of the relationship between herself and her mother and is apparently beginning to understand her mother somewhat better.

I told him that I was able to think better and that I could now "accept" my mother *as she was*. I was convinced that she couldn't change . . . but that I could. I was determined to become independent. I would listen to her demands, but I would do what I thought was best. This was a terribly difficult thing to do — something I had not been very successful at so far. My mother's disapproval, no matter how mild, had always overpowered me. But I was determined to break this pattern, and gradually I made some progress. Although each time I was with her I would sink into a slough of despond, I would deal with my feelings constructively afterward: I would substitute positive thoughts for negative ones, or listen to music I loved, or do something that would require healthy concentration.

Now I understood that although my mother no doubt meant well when she was raising me, I did have legitimate needs as a child that my mother had not met, possibly because she had been unable to meet them. But the issue really wasn't whether she couldn't or whether she wouldn't. I forgave my mother for what she may have done intentionally and for what she had done or not done unintentionally.

The wounds caused by our relationship, however, had nearly killed me, and I would always be recovering from them. In later years I would learn that these wounds would be re-opened frequently — by a word, a look, a small incident. But the pain never crippled me again.

With these realizations slowly seeping in and finding a place in my weary soul, my thoughts turned once again to my baby.

Family . . . Finally

In our households, heavenly Father,
bless the bonds that make us one.
Make our love reflect your loving,
may your will be always done.

Marie J. Post, "In Our Households,
Heavenly Father," stanza 1

To HAVE our baby daughter home had become my most important goal. Before I had dully accepted not having Anita at home as one of my failures; now getting her back had become a matter of maternal urgency. But I would have to get out of the hospital and prove myself first.

Shock treatments had again reduced my anxiety, but I still didn't feel "normal." I was very quiet and didn't socialize with other patients. And I hated the therapy room, especially "doing" handwork. (It reminded me of how much I had disappointed Ma when I hadn't learned how to knit or tat.) I tried to read, but I couldn't concentrate.

My doctor reminded me that clinical depression comes in waves. He sketched what looked like a two-lane, single-direction highway. He bisected the "highway" with a broken line. A normal person, he explained, travels forward but doesn't stay in the middle of the road. He or she is sometimes "up" in one lane, sometimes "down" in another, but always stays on the road. In fact, he or she is seldom in the middle of the road for long. "Life has many ups and downs for everybody," he said.

Next he drew another "highway" identical to the first. "Now I'll show you the path of a person who is ill with depression," he said. His pencil line started out in one lane, dropped down to the other lane, then moved onto the shoulder of the road, then went off the shoulder. Rarely did the line move back up to even the edge of the road.

What he showed me was that an emotionally healthy person does have up and down feelings but seldom feels "blue" for any length of time. An emotionally unhealthy person, however, gets bogged down in depression and sinks deeper and deeper into it, rarely rising even to the "low" of an emotionally healthy person. (People who are manic depressive, or bipolar, also struggle with abnormal highs in moods.)

Finally my doctor drew a third sketch, again beginning with the two-lane "highway," in which he showed how a person returns to mental health. In this drawing the lows were not as low, the length of the low periods shortened, and the distance between the lows increased.

He went on to say that medical scientists didn't really know just why certain people are prone to developing depression. It still represented a new challenge to the mental health field, and drugs had just recently been introduced to treat it. Depression might be caused by physical as well as emotional and psychological factors, he said; only time would tell. But at that time there had been no genuine breakthroughs.

"You mean I'll always have depression?" I asked.

"I don't know that," he said. "But as you recover, your down periods won't be as deep, won't last as long, won't come as frequently, and, I think, won't be beyond your ability to live with."

He was right.

Soon after the shock treatments were finished, I wanted to go home. At this point I had been in the hospital for six weeks. Because the children were being taken care of by relatives and I wouldn't have the immediate added stress of caring for them, and because it was almost Christmas and my doctor could tell that I was anxious to be at home for the holiday, he reluctantly agreed to let me leave the hospital, even though he noted that "when she is at home she does not seem to get well as quickly as one might expect her to get well had she been in the hospital all of the time." In his record he made these comments:

> I still believe this woman is manic depressed, depressed, but there are many schizoid appearing elements within the personality structure. She has never been frankly hallucinated or delusional. At times she seems to tend toward the paranoid and is certainly meticulous in type, demanding for herself perfection [in every area] and for others in certain spheres only. The outstanding thing has been depression.
>
> [She] was admitted this third time because of symptoms of anxiety complicated by severe depressive symptoms. It is not the usual type of depression but there is a good deal of feeling of worthlessness and hopelessness and self-accusation and generalized disinterest and flattening of feeling except on one score, which concerns her mother. . . . Condition on discharge considered only improved.

But when I got back home, I didn't continue to improve. I was tired all the time, and I said little. I felt as though I were standing outside of myself, looking at me. Reality didn't seem real. I thought I was losing my mind. Something must have happened to my brain during the past three years. Even Ray became discouraged. This was one of the down times the doctor had warned me about.

But Christmas Day itself was almost enjoyable. Ken, Donna, and Susan were with us — although Anita wasn't, and that bothered me. But I was determined not to let my regrets spoil the day. In the morning Ray took the children to the Christmas service while I stayed home. (I still hadn't overcome my fear of going to church and meeting people.)

After church our children excitedly opened their presents. I was happy to see that they behaved just like normal children: each of them tore the paper and ribbon off one package, ripped open the box and exclaimed over the gift, and then eagerly waited to open the next one. All three of them seemed very comfortable with me. Susie particularly stayed close to me. I did, I admit, shed a few tears that day, but they were tears more of gladness and thanksgiving than of sadness. (My emotions often cartwheeled between sadness and the glimmers of happiness that now and then appeared.)

We didn't visit either set of grandparents that day; I made a simple dinner for us at home. Because it was a special day, Ray and I let the children stay up later than usual. Although I was exhausted by then, I felt encouraged by my ability to "handle" — reasonably well — such an exciting day with the children.

After the holidays I went back to the hospital from time to time for outpatient shock treatments, and again my doctor changed my medicine. To my delight, this new prescription helped.

Sometime after Christmas, I went along with Ray to a church where he showed the movies he had taken while we were in Nigeria. It was a risky step, but I wanted to do it. It went well. Some of the scenes in the films were extremely painful for me to watch, but I kept my composure, and I felt a subdued triumph. With the success of this outing, I felt that one day I would be able to go back to church.

I wanted all the children back home, but most of all I wanted Anita back with us. The older children were in and out of the house much of the time, since the relatives caring for them lived nearby. My doctor suggested again that I try having one child at home at a time for periods of two or three days, and I took his suggestion. I was happy that the children wanted to be home; it felt like a personal victory. It bolstered my confidence about the possibility that I could become a mother of sorts again.

I knew that when Anita finally came home, Ray and I would practically be strangers to her, and mothering her would be taxing. I asked my doctor again if we could bring her home at this point, but he said no.

I did make progress with the other three children. Over a period of six weeks, Ken, Donna, and Susan each came home for two or three days at a time. By the middle of March, all three of them were back with us. With Ray's help in the evenings, we managed, but a less than positive pattern developed. I would hang on quite well until five p.m., but at that point I would start anxiously watching the clock until Ray came home. I counted on him for relief at night, and often I would dump my fears and worries on him. I felt a strong need to do this, but I scolded myself for it. If I could hold it together until suppertime, then why couldn't I hold it together for the rest of the night?

Meanwhile, I saw my doctor weekly. He commented on this pattern in his record of my treatment:

> This woman always wants to have things done rather patly and [wants to be] able to have things planned out for

the future. She has difficulty having things go one day at a time. . . . She says she is very much fatigued around supper time to the point where she can scarcely go on anymore. It is of some interest to note that this was her pattern last summer also even when she was at her very best. It seems as though she holds out for the day and then when her husband is around she can release the tension and have him share some of the responsibility. She does so each time.

I tried to pace myself during the day, hoping to be less tired when Ray returned from work. But usually I wasn't successful at this; I needed his help in the evening. Besides, I told myself, it was good for the children to spend time with their father too.

Toward the end of March, I again approached my doctor about bringing Anita home. In his log he made a guarded assessment of my condition: "The fact is that the patient is not much improved over what she was last time except that she appears to be a little more alert. She [needs] to force herself to do anything. Everything seems to be done because it needs to be done and not because she [takes] any pleasure in it." Still, my doctor agreed — although reluctantly, after more discussion — that if we would again get help for the summer, we could bring Anita home.

I was pleased, yet deep fear and anxiety clouded the good news. All my doubts about being able to be a good mother — especially to Anita — again crowded my mind. My doctor and I talked again, as we had many times earlier, about the danger of my "blaming" Anita for my illness. This was a potential problem because friends had sometimes mentioned that my pregnancy with Anita was a possible cause of my illness. I hadn't thought this way; rather, I had worried that Anita might be born dead or malformed, and that if she were, it would be my fault. Still, my doctor and I discussed the possibility that I might on some level blame Anita for my depression. He explained how easily we can make an *occasion* (e.g., my pregnancy) a *cause* of something. And I *had* neglected Anita so much during her first six months (while we were living in Africa) that I could easily think that I was blaming her. Talking about and clarifying the circumstances with my doctor showed me that I loved Anita dearly and could care for her.

Even so, at home, away from my doctor's encouragement, I became more frightened. Anita had excellent foster parents, an excellent foster mother — how could I possibly replace her? My husband and I discussed the matter for a few more weeks before we approached our friends about Anita's return.

When we did talk to them, we learned that Jean and John were expecting their third child! Again God had provided in his own way and in his own time; my faith was reinforced that day. We would never be able to repay John and Jean Vander-Veen for their friendship and their loving care of our baby daughter, but we were very grateful to them.

Jane Anita Grissen had been born on May 6, 1953. On May 6, 1956, she returned home to stay. At last our family was complete.

I'll never forget the first night that she was home. When I put her to bed, she looked at me. She neither cried nor smiled. I stepped away and turned toward her again, and noticed that her sober blue eyes followed me. She still didn't cry — but I did. Would she ever be "at home" with us? Would she ever love me as her mother?

I thanked God for our family, but not without some anxiety. Would we, now a complete family, be able to handle the effects of the last three years? If so, how? Would we be a "normal" family, whatever that is?

We did manage — with some help. That summer (and

the next), we had a high-school girl come in every day, Monday through Friday, to care for the children, especially Anita. Ken (now nine), Donna (now eight), and Susan (now six) were cooperative — most of the time. I rested a lot.

Even with that help, the summer wasn't easy. I was glad when September came and the children went back to school. But even though life was challenging, my will kept me struggling.

Tugging at Ties

Teach me to feel that you are always nigh;
teach me the struggles of the soul to bear,
to check the rising doubt, the rebel sigh;
teach me the patience of unceasing prayer.

"Spirit of God, Who Dwells
within My Heart," stanza 1

My DOCTOR was right when he said I would have frequent ups and downs, but he wasn't entirely right when he said I would be able to manage them. Sometimes I could, but at other times I needed to call him for reassurance. Sometimes I also made appointments to see him. Still, although I leaned on him heavily, during the next three years I saw him less and less. He commented on my progress in an entry he made in February 1958 after I had had a session with him:

> This former inpatient, who has been doing unusually well and living a very well-adjusted life for the past two years,

came in today stating . . . she wonders whether [she is experiencing] the beginning of a new depression.

The mechanism of a depression and the up and down wavelike emotions of a depression are gone over with her. Various factors involved are once again gone into with her by way of review.

She is a very understanding person. She has learned a great deal about psychiatric principles and she has a great deal of insight into herself. She is utterly honest, and she states at the end of the interview that she sees things a good deal differently, even though she now has to face the fact that she is going into another depressive episode, which at the present time she recognizes as being very mild.

No medication is given to her at this time.

As my doctor's assessment indicates, my depression varied in intensity. And sometimes it hit me for reasons I couldn't identify. Like the breaking surf of a wild ocean, it knocked me over, but I never drowned again. I never lost hope. I was learning to live with my own limitations. All my life I had fought without knowing what I was fighting against. Now I knew the enemies. I not only had to reconcile myself to them; I had to become friends with them. I learned to think about what I was planning to do, not dwell on what I had already done.

Although I sometimes couldn't trace my depression to a specific cause, often it was triggered by some request or demand of my mother. As I look back now, I realize that my relationship with my mother until the time of her death figured very importantly in three events — ones that indicate how, over time, I came to terms with the biggest single challenge in my life.

I

The tension between my mother and me continued, and her requirements of me — or shall I say demands — made Ray and me think often of my doctor's question, "What do you do if you live in a flood plain?"

In 1959 my family and I decided to move to Phoenix, Arizona, to get away from the frequently overflowing banks. Ray and I wanted to see if physical separation from my mother would lighten the burden of my repeated bouts with depression. Our children were excited about the move, but Ma was bitter. She cried, asked why we were leaving, and tried to convince us that we shouldn't move away from her. Hadn't she moved to the north end of town just to be near me? I reminded her — although it was difficult for me to do so — that she had put an ocean between herself and her parents even before she was married when she had followed her fiancé (my father) to Canada.

With this move the ties between my mother and me were stretched, but they weren't broken. I had forgiven her, but I couldn't forget the past when both her letters and her phone calls reminded me how much I displeased her. Even long-distance contact with her was difficult for me: sometimes I had an anxiety attack; sometimes I slipped into a struggle with depression that lasted for days. At other times I would get so fatigued that I would have no zest for living. It surprised me how much control my mother exercised over me, even from more than 2,500 miles away. True, I was better equipped to discard what I neither needed nor wanted in the relationship, but it took both effort and energy. And physical distance didn't always separate me and Ma. My parents frequently spent from six to twelve weeks with us during the winter. Any pain that I felt I kept inside me during these weeks, although after they left I paid the price in another bout of extreme fatigue and depression. The visits themselves went well, but I always needed some time to recover from them.

II

It was September 1978. It was a sunny Saturday morning in Denver, where my family and I had been living for three years. What ended up being a transforming experience for me began with a phone call from a dear friend who lived in Flagstaff, Arizona. "Lil," she said, excitedly, "I've found such a good book for you. You have to read it."

The book my friend referred to was Nancy Friday's *My Mother, My Self: The Daughter's Search for Identity.* I dropped the work I was doing, hurried to the bookstore, and bought the recently released hardback. When I got home, I curled up in my chair in our warm and sunny east room and read the book from cover to cover. I couldn't put it down. My friend's recommending this particular book showed how well she understood me and my problems.

After reading this best-seller, I felt like Christian in *Pilgrim's Progress.* Although he believed he had been forgiven, he still carried the burden of his sin on his back. By the time I finished the book, the "burden" I carried had rolled off my back — not the burden of sin but the nagging question of how thoroughly I had forgiven my mother. I had been forgiving her for many years, little by little. Forgiveness had been a process for me, not a single act. But forgetting was something I hadn't been able to do — and that had troubled me.

When I read this book I learned why, in spite of having forgiven my mother for what I considered to be her unfairness and sometimes her cruelty toward me as a child, I couldn't forget the emotional crippling I had experienced — even though I tried. For the first time I *understood* why I continued to notice the effects of my childhood in my life. Even more important, I felt I understood *her.* Just like me, my mother was the *result* of the way she had been brought up. Mothers teach daughters from generation to generation. Ma too had been taught that her role was to be a wife and mother — the Bible taught this, she had been taught this, and that was it. The pattern had been set generations ago and had been passed along to me.

I considered all the limitations Ma faced. She was a foreigner in a strange country. She was without the support system of her birth family. She had only the deeply ingrained rigidity of her own traditional, Calvinistic upbringing to guide her, without the benefit of any liberating education. Under the circumstances, Ma couldn't help but perpetuate what she had learned in childhood.

Friday's book lacks a Christian foundation, so I have some reservations about its ability to enlighten those Christians who, expecting a clear Christian viewpoint, might fail to see its value. But I recommend it nonetheless. It deals realistically with the complexity of mother-daughter relationships, and it clearly shows how these relationships, whether they're Christian or not, can become tension-filled, and how daughters can unknowingly perpetuate the ideas and behaviors they learned from their mothers.

I cried and thanked God for Friday's book. I would have liked to have called Ma and discussed it with her, but I knew that she wouldn't, couldn't have understood it. I found this somewhat frustrating. But even after reading this book, I was still deeply thankful that I had never confronted her about our relationship. And now I noticed that I felt a gentleness, almost a tenderness toward Ma that I hadn't experienced before. I found myself wishing that she could have had the same help that I had enjoyed; she was an intelligent woman, and I know she would have benefited from it.

I don't mean to suggest that reading this book suddenly and magically created the kind of circumstance so often described in Christian books — where the mother and daughter suddenly open up to each other, instantly develop intimacy, and enjoy a close companionship. Because life is gray, the perfect relationship between my mother and me must wait until heaven. Our relationship here on earth was like a broken leg that has been set imperfectly. The leg itself mends, but the imperfection remains.

III

I will never forget seeing Ma in her casket. She died in July 1989, just three months short of her ninety-eighth birthday. (Pa had died fourteen years earlier.) I saw on her face a peace, a heavenly peace, that I had never seen before. She was now with her Lord.

I'm glad that I was sad.

My mind wandered back over the last several years. Seven years before, Ray and I had returned to Grand Rapids. I had felt that with my greatly increased understanding of some of the reasons for the difficulties I had experienced, the "floodwaters," as my doctor had called them, had receded greatly.

But the rain still fell often. Ma domineered until the last smidgin of her energy was gone. She couldn't resist reprimanding and correcting her daughter; I was still her child. Often on my way to visit her, I would tell myself to be strong, but she frequently succeeded in making me wince under her disapproval. Even now, it pained me to disappoint her.

During her last few years, as her strength and spirit ebbed, she couldn't reconcile the weakness that had overtaken her with her image of herself. A safety harness that strapped her to her bed in the nursing home was her jailer. I pitied this strong woman, reduced to the captivity of frailty. She hated what being old did to her. What she had said to me for as long as I could remember she said until a few weeks before her death: *"Ja, meid,* someday you'll see. . . ."

Toward the end, she longed for death. Although she often doubted, she remained a believer. Until she could not, she prayed for her children, her grandchildren, her great-grandchildren, and the missionaries. Until she could not, she gave to the church and its many ministries of mercy.

I loved that woman who was my mother, and although I wouldn't have wanted her to suffer with depression as I had, it grieved me that she had not in her lifetime experienced being broken by Almighty God as I had. I thought of John Donne's immortal sonnet:

> Batter my heart, three person'd God; for you
> As yet but knock, breathe, shine, and seek to mend;
> That I may rise and stand, o'erthrow me and bend
> Your force, to break, blow, burn and make me new.
> I, like an usurped town, to another due,
> Labor to admit you, but Oh, to no end;
> Reason, your viceroy in me, me should defend,
> But is captived and proves weak or untrue.
> Yet dearly I love you and would be loved fain,
> But am betrothed unto your enemy:
> Divorce me, untie or break that knot again,
> Take me to you, imprison me, for I
> Except you enthrall me, never shall be free,
> Nor ever chaste, except you ravish me.

I visited Ma one hot July day, shortly before my husband and I left on a vacation. I didn't know it would be my last good-bye to her, nor did she. She lay in bed, more than half asleep. I bent over and whispered, "Ma, do you know who I am?"

"*Ja,*" she whispered weakly, "Anna." Anna was one of Ma's sisters. I didn't correct her, but my eyes filled with tears. I kissed her gently, twice, as I held her bony hand.

"Good-bye, Ma. Good-bye. God bless you, Ma." Her eyes opened a bit, then closed. Did she hear me? I don't know. I turned, walked away, and didn't look back.

Three days later she died. At first I felt nothing. Later, when I saw her in her coffin, I couldn't stop crying, yet the tears didn't help. I examined my feelings. I felt empty; the earthly relationship between my mother and me was now over, and it had been troubled to the end.

Should I have confronted Ma with my complaints? No, I decided, I was glad I hadn't hurt her in that way, at least. But I had disappointed her in so many ways. Had I failed to do some things for her that I *could* have done? I had forgiven her totally, but my pain had returned.

I felt no guilt, only grief. I had kept my vow not to burden Ma's old age with my perceptions (and misperceptions, perhaps) of her feelings for me. I regretted that she had never had the daughter she wanted. We had tiptoed in a relationship that invites dancing. We had said little when we could have fellow-shipped. We had talked when we could have embraced.

At first my grief puzzled me, but then suddenly I understood it: I was grieving for a kind of mother-daughter relationship that had never existed between Ma and me. She had wanted me to love her, and in my own way I had. I had wanted her to love me too, and in her own way, she had. Yet, in this flawed life, we had never connected.

Now she was dead and in heaven, and I was alive on earth.

My soul was desolate. The mystery of our nonrelationship

haunted me for a few weeks. Our relationship was one of blood, even of love and oneness in Jesus Christ, but neither of us had known the bond of a healthy mother-daughter relationship.

Never before had I seen so clearly that life is neither black nor white but gray. I was glad that Ma was now with her Lord. In heaven she would no longer have to judge what was evil and what was good; there she would experience only good.

The relationship my mother and I did have hasn't ended, but it has changed. It isn't without flaws, but it is on its way. The ascended half of the relationship has now been perfected. The other half must wait until we meet in heaven.

My family worried as I continued to grieve over Ma's death. My daughters did their best to comfort me — and made some very wise observations in the process. "Mom," Anita said, "don't forget that you, Grandma, and I are alike. You and I have had help. Grandma never did." And Donna said, "Mom, don't forget — she's not your mother now; she's your sister."

Yes, Ma has found peace, and yes, I have peace. It is the peace of God, and it passes understanding. At least mine.

Yes, There Is Life after Depression

Come, everyone who loves the Lord,
hear what he did for me.
My cry for help has turned to praise,
for he has set me free.

Marie J. Post, "Come, Everyone,
and Join with Us," stanza 5 (Psalm 66)

MOVING TO Phoenix in 1959 did indeed give us a new start. Neither Ray nor I had ever been in Phoenix, but our experience in Nigeria encouraged us to choose a warm climate. Ray, always the adventurer, assured me that the road to Phoenix ran two ways; if we didn't like it there, we could move back to Grand Rapids or try another place.

During the first few years we lived in Phoenix, I called my doctor only twice. When Dr. Van Noord died in 1962, I was at first overwhelmed by a wave of anxiety, but gradually I overcame the loneliness of knowing he wasn't "as near as the telephone," as he had assured me he would be when we left Grand Rapids.

Shortly after we moved, I registered for my first college-level English course taught via television. It was a course in creative writing. The professor explained and lectured on television and required that students turn in one written assignment per week. This time I successfully completed the class, and I did get college credit. I was thrilled.

I knew now that I could do college-level studying, and I wanted to take another course. Ray encouraged me to continue, so I went to night school and summer school. In the early sixties, because there was a shortage of teachers in the local Christian school, I was given a contract to teach fifth and sixth grade, even though I had barely two years of college education. At last my childhood dream of being a teacher was fulfilled.

After teaching for three years, I enrolled full-time at Arizona State University, and in 1968 I graduated summa cum laude, with a bachelor of arts degree in English.

By this time (1968), Ken and Donna were in college, Susan was working, and Anita was in high school. At this point we moved to Denver, where my husband became the plant superintendent of Bethesda Hospital. I taught seventh- and eighth-grade English and Bible classes for several years in a local Christian school, and also began writing curriculum materials. In addition, I started to do some public speaking — about Christian education, remedial reading, my illness, and, later on, biblical feminism and spiritual topics. In 1976 I also accepted the editorship of the *Christian Educators Journal,* a professional magazine for Christian teachers. I held this position for six years in addition to my teaching job.

When my family and I lived in Denver, I pursued a master's degree at the University of Colorado. In September 1975 I was given a semester's leave of absence from the school where I was teaching in order to finish my course work. During that time, Ray and I and five other couples sponsored a Chinese family who had escaped from Vietnam. For a few months, members of the extended family lived with us — up to fifteen people at one time — which made it difficult for me to find the time — and a quiet place — to study at home. Knowing that this frustrated me, Ray suggested that I live in a motel from Monday to Friday in order to concentrate on my studies. I took his suggestion, so during the week he hosted the Chinese, enjoying the cooking and the attention of the seven adult women in the family. On the weekends I came home and enjoyed myself with my husband and our new friends. This arrangement worked: in December I received a master of arts degree in journalism.

Everything was going so well. Surely, I believed, I could now "handle" depression no matter what. All I had to do was follow the general rules for mental health. Right?

Wrong.

It happened in 1978, during our last year in Denver. I had been having some personal problems, as any normal person has from time to time in his or her life. I began to feel very vulnerable again. I thought I had learned to separate criticism of my work from criticism of me, but I discovered that I had to relearn this lesson. I wasn't ready for the severe bout with depression that pulled me down to such a low point that I couldn't teach for a week. I started thinking that I would have to go to a psychiatrist for help; if I didn't, I might have to be hospitalized again. In fact, I did consult a psychiatrist, and he turned out to be a good choice; he had worked with many teachers in the Denver public school system. He gave me a relatively new medicine, which helped me resume my regular work schedule while he helped me work through my depression. I wasn't completely well when I left this doctor's care when my family and I moved back to Phoenix. But once in Phoenix I consulted a psychiatrist recommended by my doctor in Denver.

By this time the psychiatric field had made great strides in treating certain disorders with drugs. Researchers had learned that a chemical imbalance in the brain could be as major a cause of depression as psychiatric problems, and a number of drugs were now being used to correct such imbalances. The doctor in Phoenix who had been recommended to me was a strong believer in the new medicines. After briefly reviewing my past treatment with me, he wrote for my case history from Pine Rest. He said he was convinced that one of the new drugs would help me. He experimented with different drugs and dosages, and after eleven months, he gave me a prescription that erased depression from my life . . . and has continued to do so up to the present time.

Sometime later, in the spring of 1979, the president of a small college in Iowa invited my husband and me to consider accepting positions there. (By now our children were adults and living on their own.) We decided to take the jobs, and we moved to Sioux Center. Ray supervised the students who receive a stipend toward tuition, and I served as an assistant professor of English for three years.

When Ray retired in 1982, he and I returned to Grand Rapids. Although my mother was still living, I no longer felt the need to keep physical distance between her and me. Six months after we came back to Grand Rapids, I was appointed to the position of associate editor of our denomination's weekly magazine, where I worked until my retirement.

Throughout these years, on every application and in every interview, I have purposely called attention to my having been hospitalized for mental illness. Although the darkest days of my depression were difficult to live through, my experience with depression has been an asset and a blessing. Among other things, it has improved my ability to understand others. Only twice have I run into difficulty: I was refused a driver's license in Denver, a decision that I contested (and won), and I was refused automobile insurance with a particular company. Ray and I simply bought our insurance from another carrier.

God's path for me was through the sea, his way through the mighty waters, and his footprints I could not see (Ps. 77:19). But he was with me all the way. I was just too mixed up to see him and feel his nearness for a time.

Yes, there is life after depression. And for me it is far more abundant than it was before. God's ways are mysterious — and wonderful.

O use me, Lord, use even me,
just as you will, and when, and where
until your blessed face I see,
your rest, your joy, your glory share.

"Lord, Speak to Me, That
I May Speak," stanza 4

Afterword

God moved in a mysterious way
his wonders to perform;
He planted footsteps in the sea,
and rode upon my storm.
Deep in unfathomable mines
of never-failing skill,
he treasured up his bright designs
and worked his sovereign will.

THIS PERSONALIZED paraphrase of the first two verses of a very familiar hymn, written by William Cowper in 1772, describes the path on which God transformed me from victim to victor in my battle with clinical depression.

An emotionally healthy Christian life is a joyful mystery. I am no longer an emotionally fragmented person, although remnants of my old self do of course bob up from time to time in the energetic life of the new me.

Today I live differently and use a different standard to assess myself. I experience God's grace, which Dietrich Bonhoeffer has described as free but not cheap. Now I find that sorrows, problems, reversals, disappointments, suffering, and decision-making are less anxiety-producing. I feel less anxious in large part because I have learned, with the psalmist, that God himself through Jesus Christ hems me in, behind and before, and keeps his hand upon me (139:5-6). I now can say with Paul, "I know what it is to be in need, and I know what it is to have plenty" (Phil. 4:12).

Mental health? Yes.

Emotional health? Yes.

Spiritual health? Yes.

God used my deep depression — mental, emotional, and spiritual — to bless me richly. I would not have grown nearly as much if he had prevented me from banging my head, my heart, and my spirit against immovable barriers. My breakdown was God's breakthrough.

I don't know when Jesus Christ will come for me. But I do know that it will be when his work in and through me is finished. Until then, my gratitude to God will continue abundantly.

Understanding Depression

Curing depression requires properly diagnosing and treating *all* components of the patient's depression. Dr. Janice Wood Wetzel, a clinician, researcher, and consultant in the treatment and study of depression, is the author of the *Clinical Handbook of Depression*. In this book she points out that "while differing theories view depression from a number of varying perspectives, when analyzed their commonalities also become clear. Psychological, sociological, biochemical, and even spiritual deficits may impact on well-being." Each individual is unique and may suffer from one or more elements of depression. It is indeed a disease of *deficits*. My illness embraced all of them.

It still hurts to hear Christians belittle the work of Christian psychiatrists, psychologists, social workers, and other therapists. Too often people hesitate to consult mental health professionals. And too often well-meaning Christians believe that God and prayer are the answers, if only you have faith. Yes, make yourself right with God, they say, and everything will be fine. One parent I know told his daughter that she would go to hell unless she changed. Little do these earnest people realize that psychological crippling can also impair a person's spiritual health. A whole, happy, healthy Christian will enjoy spiritual well-being. But a Christian who is emotionally unwell may also be suffering from spiritual ill health.

This is why professional help is so important. The professional therapist notes what areas seem to cause the patient the most pain and helps the patient to talk about it as he is able. Sometimes the source of the pain is buried so deeply within the patient that he can't remember it. In these cases the professional performs the particularly valuable service of helping the patient gradually unearth the root of the problem.

The treatment of depression has changed a great deal since I underwent therapy in the 1950s. Today group therapy has replaced some individual therapy, and rather than hospitalizing a patient, doctors try to treat her on an outpatient basis, in this way keeping her in the community. When a person is hospitalized today, often a team — made up of a psychiatrist, a psychologist, a social worker, a therapist of one sort or another, a nurse, a chaplain, a group facilitator, and possibly others — determines the best treatment for the patient. In earlier decades, hospitalization often lasted months; today, because of different and improved forms of treatment, the average stay lasts from three to six weeks.

Usually (though not always) a person will display certain symptoms which suggest that she or he is experiencing depression serious enough that she or he must consider consulting a doctor. Although symptoms vary, probably the first observable one is *change*. The person afflicted acts different and *is* different in one or more ways. He may go from being energetic to being sleepy all the time, or vice versa. She may overeat or undereat. He may go from "workaholism" to full-time idleness. A "morning person" may begin to feel bad in the morning but better toward evening; a "night person" might experience the reverse pattern. If a person undergoes two or more of these changes in feelings or behavior for a period of more than two or three weeks, he or she may need help.

But then there's the stigma of consulting a psychiatrist. Some people run to a physician with the first sniffle or twinge; others are more stoical. Some go with a stomachache; others wait until their appendix bursts. Still, consulting a doctor about a physical problem is a common and socially accepted practice. But visit a psychiatrist — a medical doctor who has studied at least three more years for a diploma in psychiatry? No. A person would rather suffer in excruciating silence than be embarrassed, even humiliated, by consulting a "shrink"! Diagnosis and medication from a doctor? Yes. From a psychiatrist? No. Not on your *life!* And that's exactly what is involved — one's emotional, physical, and spiritual life.

And there is not only the stigma attached to psychiatric treatment; there is also the challenge and uncertainty of treatment. A physician may be able to give a patient a shot or some pills that alleviate his or her physical condition. Unfortunately, however, depression can't be cured by a doctor's ten-day prescription. Even today the disease remains mysterious, and research continues.

Deep depression involves every aspect of a person's being. That becomes clear when we look at some of its components.

1. Sadness. As a cocoon envelops a larva, so sadness enshrouds a depressed person. Just as clothing stored in a cedar closet takes on that odor, so a depressed person, almost by osmosis, absorbs sadness. It permeates his whole being — the mind, the body, the heart, the spirit. Its extreme tenacity makes it impossible to shrug off or "get over."

2. Fatigue. I wish there were another term for this feeling, because *fatigue* is far too mild a word to describe what the depressed person experiences. The fatigue of depression is frequently misunderstood. I once heard a minister-counselor make this pronouncement: "The young lady claimed she couldn't do the ironing. 'I can't iron,' she said; 'I'm too tired.' Too often 'I can't' means 'I won't.' All she needs to do is put the plug of the iron in the socket and begin." No, no, no! I doubt whether that man has ever personally experienced depression. To this woman, the laundry pile looks as high as Mount Everest, the iron weighs a ton, and her arm is like a piece of wet string, so *doing* the ironing is impossible. When one's jaw is too tired to move, and when the trip from fork to mouth is as far as from earth to outer space, even eating a fresh lettuce salad becomes impossible. The fatigue of depression puts one in a state of constant exhaustion; it is severely debilitating because it renders one almost motionless.

3. *Mental pain.* William Styron is a Pulitzer prize-winning author. He is also someone who suffers from depression. A few years ago he published a brief account of his experience with depression called *Darkness Visible,* in which he attempts to describe the mental anguish of depression by explaining how he felt at one low point:

> I was feeling in my mind a sensation close to, but indescribably different from, actual pain. . . . That the word "indescribable" should present itself is not fortuitous, since it has to be emphasized that if the pain were readily describable most of the countless sufferers from this ancient affliction would have been able to confidently depict for their friends and loved ones (even their physicians) some of the actual dimensions of their torment, and perhaps elicit a comprehension that has been generally lacking.

Styron is right: the pain of depression is beyond description. Sometimes sympathetic well-wishers may say to someone who's experiencing depression, "Yes, I know. I get depressed once in a while too." But these people are making a false connection. They do not and cannot know what this pain is like unless they have experienced the illness of clinical depression. The contractions of childbirth are more bearable than the pain of depression.

4. *Loneliness.* Depressed people are often lonely without being able to articulate the feeling, even to themselves. A depressed person will say, "You just don't understand," which is usually true because depression is understood best by people who have experienced it.

This loneliness creates an awful emptiness that, unlike a vacuum, cannot be filled — by anyone. Death suggests itself not as a remedy but as a final solution.

5. *Anxiety.* For many reasons, usually trivial, waves of anxiety wash over the depressed person, and he feels like he's drowning. Anxiety is often exhibited in a range of physiological symptoms, such as sweating, restlessness, headaches, and increased pulse. When I was hospitalized, I remember, one patient shook so violently that the bed moved with her. Anxiety produces fear, and fear produces anxiety. Together they form a powerful kinship that cannot be reasoned away. Anxiety causes brooding, and brooding too increases anxiety. Dr. Abraham Low, the founder of Recovery, Inc., and the author of *Mental Health through Will Training,* attributes anxiety to imagination that is on fire, which "produces the sense of . . . insecurity." This saps a person's energy, and this fatigue in turn makes certain common tasks seem like huge challenges. Decision making is one of them. The depressed person might begin to invest small decisions with great importance: very small matters such as what kind of shoes or socks to buy for a child may be more worrisome than whether the doctor's fees will be covered by insurance. Because of her misperception of the process, the depressed person can be paralyzed by decision making.

6. *Self-tyranny.* When thoroughly confused thoughts control a depressed person, they demand both total time and total energy. There is no escape, no letup, no relief. In his inimitable way, Rev. J. D. Eppinga, a retired minister in my denomination, once wrote of the awful pain he felt when he first slammed the car door on his thumb and later got stung on his ear by a bee:

> The rest of the day was *a total loss.* I lay on a wicker couch on the porch, entirely bereft of my zest for life. I wondered whether it might be prudent to cancel my engagement [two preaching services] the next day. *Would I be able to put my mind on anything but my wounds?* (*The Banner,* 12 October 1991, my emphasis)

A crushed thumb and a bee sting cause pain to the body just as depression causes pain to the heart. But that's where the comparison stops. The pain of physical injuries like the ones Eppinga describes begins to subside after several hours or a day, and they become less and less distracting. But depression takes as prisoner all your thoughts and emotions day and night, and it lasts much longer than a day — sometimes weeks, sometimes months or years. You are unable to put your mind on anything else. There is nothing you would rather do, but often you simply can't.

7. *Meaninglessness.* What is meaninglessness? you ask. Life holds different meanings for different people; depression robs a person of all the significant meanings that make life worthwhile for her. For me, life had meaning because of the involvement of my self or my psyche as an image bearer of God, a woman in relationship to Almighty God, saved to serve him (through family, church, and community) and enjoy him. When all of that disappeared in despair, life became meaningless for me.

8. *Guilt and shame.* Shame often prevents a person from

sharing her disease with others. Shame, coupled with guilt, often cannot be tied directly to a specific action (or lack of it). Although it may be nonspecific and nebulous, the guilt *feeling* is tragically real. It can be especially difficult for the Christian who has been taught that "God is only a prayer away," because guilt makes him feel estranged from God. Sometimes the person cries — pleading or accusing — to the god who doesn't seem to hear, the god who doesn't seem to be there.

Guilt and shame — depression's cancerous couple — differ greatly. Guilt says, "I have made a mistake" or "I have sinned." Shame shouts, "I *am* a mistake" or "I *am* sin." In combination they can make an individual misperceive self and reality.

Guilt can be true or false. Dr. O. Quentin Hyder, author of *The Christian's Handbook of Psychiatry,* writes that "false guilt is somewhat of a misnomer. It is a useful term because it is short." He quotes the clarification offered by Dr. Paul Tournier, a noted Christian psychiatrist, who calls false guilt *functional guilt*, and goes on to distinguish it from true guilt: "A feeling of *functional guilt* is one which results from social suggestion, fear of taboos, or of losing the love of others. . . . that which comes as a result of the judgments and suggestions of men. 'True guilt' is that which results from divine judgment."

A depressed individual needs Christian doctors, ministers, nurses, and therapists to reintroduce the compassionate love of a merciful God to his reality. Disentangling the distortions produced by guilt and shame requires delicacy, diligence, and professional wisdom.

9. *Worthlessness.* A depressed person's biggest enemy is her "guilty" and "shameful" self — the harsh and distorted judgments it makes. "I'm not worth a nickel." "I'm of no use to anyone." "My family would be better off if I were dead." Self-torture has displaced self-esteem. It has flown out of the heart's window; an ugly nothingness has stormed in.

For Christians, Calvinist Christians especially, the mistaken idea that human beings are worthless and full of sin and the fear of having committed the "unforgivable sin" are sometimes crushing. Depression causes many of these sufferers to deny personal spiritual safety and embrace worthlessness with a vengeance. Rejected by God and guilty of committing the unforgivable sin — does anything worthwhile remain?

10. Self-destruction. Despair sometimes makes the depressed person apathetic to or incapable of following general health rules regarding eating, sleeping, exercising, and sometimes personal cleanliness. These are all forms of self-neglect and self-destruction on a smaller scale; in extreme cases, depression can drive an individual to suicide.

During the Great Depression, a Christian, church-attending father hanged himself in his barn. He had been a "strange person" for a long time, I overheard people say, and "never did work very hard" on his farm. I was about ten or eleven, and my friends and I whispered about it. I got very scared when I learned that the man went to hell. One of my classmates told me that grownups called suicide the "unforgivable sin." I no longer believe that. Christians whose emotions have been brutally terrorized by depression and who commit suicide out of terrible desperation are not removed from the Great Physician's compassion and eternal healing. God understands depression. A mentally healthy Christian does not believe suicide is an invitation to heaven, of course. But neither is it a doorway to hell.

11. Hopelessness. The very worst part of depression is the absence of hope. Helplessness easily slips into hopelessness. It is the essence of depression. All is waste and void. There is no out, no exit. The self has fallen and broken into thousands of pieces, and no one will ever be able to put this Humpty Dumpty together again. The depressed person does not lie at the bottom of the sea; he lies beneath the bottom.

Does God reach into the bowels of the sea to save this person? The depressed person doesn't think so; in his eyes, God has turned his back. Why would he belittle himself by stooping to such depths?

Not all those who suffer the disease of depression suffer from all these negative emotions, of course, nor are the degrees of suffering the same. Yet someone who is suffering from even two or three of these ugly distortions can be in a great deal of pain — pain that can be greatly relieved with the help of competent psychiatric professionals.

Where and how do such sick, disturbing thoughts originate? How does such cancer of the emotions take hold? The search for reasons and causes continues. One breakthrough in recent years is the recognition of the biochemical causes of depression, and many sufferers have received help through drugs.

Depression can be ascribed to either psychological or biological causes and often to both. Sometimes it is difficult to tell which precipitates what. Some researchers say that when there is a biochemical change in the brain, depression can result. Others say that depression seems to create the chemical imbalance. Each feeds the other, and the sick person becomes sicker. Research on both causes is continuing. To operate normally, the brain requires a certain number of neurotransmitters, which are chemical substances that transmit nerve impulses. When the brain is deficient in two of these chemicals, norepinephrine and serotonin, depression occurs. Research is demonstrating that a shortage of neurotransmitters is something that can be inherited genetically. The tendency to have this deficit can run in families, as it has in mine.

Clearly, the causes and sources of depression are not simple, nor are they always easily discernible by the sufferer or the doctor. Sometimes experiencing a great loss — the loss of a spouse, a child, a job, one's possessions, one's health — can bring on a sudden attack. And living in a destructive emotional environment for even a limited time can harm a person of any age and trigger depression. But often the causes of depression build over a long period of time. Sometimes the event of the moment is blamed when actually it is merely the spark that ignites a fire that has long been smoldering.

The source can reach back as far as childhood, and often it does. In the Parable of the Weeds, found in Matthew 13:24-29, both the weeds and the wheat "sprouted and formed heads" (v. 26). The fertile ground nourished both. Children are an especially fertile ground for planting — and they too nurture both wheat and weeds, since they only slowly devleop the ability to distinguish between them. Parents, frail and human, are the planters, and they do not plant only wheat, but it is difficult for children to recognize this. To them, parents are gods, and what they do and say is right. Most children become healthy adults and are able to winnow the weeds from the wheat. Others, like me, need help — first in separating the wheat from the weeds, and then in pulling out the weeds and nurturing the healthy wheat.

Dr. William E. Van Eerden, a psychiatrist at Pine Rest Christian Hospital, explains a frequent cause of depression:

> Psychological depressions . . . are generally caused by life stress. Commonly depression is a response to loss. People lose something they need to maintain their sense of well-being. Separation from a spouse, close friend, or a valued work associate — whether through death or for other reasons — may bring about depression. So may loss of physical health, financial security, or self-esteem.
>
> The causes of depression may also come from within rather than from the environment. When people bottle up

unresolved anger through repression and denial, they may cause depression. Any emotion has a tendency to convert itself into a harmful force if it is not expressed in some way. (*Pine Rest Today,* Fall 1991, p. 1)

In *The Dance of Anger: A Woman's Guide to Changing the Patterns of Intimate Relationships,* Harriet Goldhar Lerner explains how unresolved anger can affect women: "Feelings of depression, low self-esteem, and even self-hatred are inevitable when we fight but continue to submit to unfair circumstances, when we complain but live in a way that betrays our hopes, values and potentials, or when we find ourselves fulfilling society's stereotype of the bitchy, nagging, bitter, or destructive woman."

One can also break down from unrelenting frustration and lack of fulfillment. Women who feel trapped in limiting circumstances sometimes feel helpless, although often they are not able or don't dare to articulate this feeling even to themselves. When I was in the hospital, I was surprised that so many of the women were young like me. Most of us had children, some as young as mine. Many of these women, I learned — not only I — fidgeted and even became weary with two or three or more little ones to take care of all day. On top of that, some found their evenings taken up by providing and caring for their husbands. "Who takes care of me?" such women ask — but then feel guilty for raising the question. Women caught in this struggle need to learn that their frustrations are legitimate, and that they have a right to express them and need to look for ways to address them.

Although the symptoms of depression are similar for many people, the specific sources of depression can and do vary greatly from person to person. Most people suffering from clinical depression need help in identifying these sources. Only then can they begin to rebuild their shattered mental health.

Today much can be and is being done to help people who suffer from clinical depression. Medical doctors often prescribe antidepressants and anxiety-reducing drugs, but if an individual doesn't experience relief within a reasonable period of time, he or she should contact a specialist — in this case, a psychiatrist.

Often psychiatrists will prescribe medicine that will bring the biochemicals of the brain into balance. Beginning to use antidepressant medicines as well as stopping their use or adjusting the dosage requires the supervision of a doctor (preferably a psychiatrist). Long after I had started taking medication, I learned that a reduction of only twenty-five milligrams of an antidepressant soon affected my chemical equilibrium and emotional well-being.

A minister once said, "Some people think they can cure all their problems by taking a drug." That was an unfortunate remark which suggested that drug use was drug abuse. It is this kind of thinking that can keep a depressed person from taking the drugs he or she really needs. And it's as foolish for a depressed person to refuse to take an antidepressant that can restore equilibrium to the brain as it is foolish for a diabetic to refuse insulin.

No one is immune from depression. It has many faces, and it strikes all kinds of personalities, although some are more susceptible than others. That it has genetic roots is generally accepted today. Some people who experience deep depression do become well and functional without psychiatric or chemical help. Still, with competent Christian therapy, a person not only can get well but also can learn to lead a richer, fuller life.

Such has been my experience. God's path led me through the sea, and I didn't see his footprints. But I know now that he was with me all the way.

APPENDIX B

A Husband Looks at Depression

Raymond Grissen

ONE ENGINE of our plane had stopped. A few minutes later, a second engine of the four-engine prop plane stopped. This fits in with the rest of the events of the last few days, I thought. The words of the doctor at Lupwe, Nigeria, rang in my ears: "Take your children and your wife back to the States. She needs more help than we can give her here."

My wife and children wore summer clothes appropriate for the warmth of Lupwe; now, as we prepared to land in Newfoundland, the attendants wrapped them in warm blankets. Our lives are falling apart, I thought. We had four very young children. My wife was tormented with devastating fatigue, a chronic, severe headache, and a deep despair that made living a chore. We had said our farewells to friends, white and black, whom we had learned to love. I was giving up building, supervising, and teaching construction to young African men — a task that challenged me.

Why does God let things like this happen?

At first I thought Lil and I just needed a vacation, just the two of us, away from our busy children, away from everyone. But no. Not a vacation, the doctor said. "She's sick, and her sickness will go with you wherever you go." I was to learn, slowly, that my wife's problems were deep-rooted, that they had been developing for a long time, and that they would take much effort, more help, and even a longer time to overcome.

Learning bit by bit. Missionaries can't come home from Africa ahead of schedule without people wondering what had happened to them. Was it a disgrace? How much could one say about fatigue, headache, and despondency? Would people understand? I learned a few did and more didn't. It became possible for me to talk about it rather than hide it after I had grappled with my own feelings and accepted the fact that my wife wasn't *just* tired and feeling blue. She was very sick. Depression — or clinical depression, as it is more accurately called — *is* sickness. It needs to be treated by a doctor, a psychiatrist. For my wife, especially because her depression included spiritual dilemmas, a *Christian* psychiatrist was a must.

I soon realized that her illness affected and controlled our entire family. She was barely aware of what was happening. Her depression and the medicine, shock treatments, and therapy used to treat it all reduced to a minimum her engagement with our family — her interest, involvement, energy, and concern. Lil was hospitalized for several months, and I visited her regularly, almost every day. These visits were often tense, difficult, and short. Even family and friends weren't comfortable around us. I listened to much well-meant advice — about cheering her up, about remedies, about raising children, and more. I soon learned to listen quietly and to keep reminding myself that each case was different. I had to make my own decisions, alone, many of them.

At times I grew angry. At other times I became discouraged, lonely, or just plain sick of everything, especially when it took months to see even slight progress, only to see it disappear in a setback. But I learned too to allow myself my feelings, and gradually I became more open and honest about myself, my wife's illness, its complex causes — and the long road ahead.

Hindsight, of course, is 20/20. Both Lil and I say now that had we known, had we seen ahead of time what we learned during her illness, some — though not all — of it might have been prevented. We would have sought help sooner not only for some of the symptoms but also for some of the problems that had surfaced earlier to varying degrees. True, when my wife was ill, knowledge of depression as a disease was much more limited than it is today. In spite of that, however, we could have been spared some of our pain had we been able to see and admit that many people, including Christians, have problems that can cause emotional upsets, nervous breakdowns, or clinical depression.

No two situations, no two illnesses are identical, but the same God cares for us all. Sometimes people — especially Christians — are afraid to seek help because they're afraid that others will see their flaws, because they're afraid of what others will think. We too felt that way — until it happened to us.

Pastoral help. Some ministers realize that depression is a disease; many do not. Sharing the hospital room with my wife was a woman also existing in the black pit of despair. Her minister, intending to cheer her, said, "No one has ever died from this." She replied bitterly, "I know. I wish I could." Equally disastrous is the minister's well-meant advice to a depressed person to lay her burdens before the Lord in order to find peace for her soul. The person desperately wishes she could, but she can't. Preaching is not a helpful prescription. Does a minister comfort a person suffering from cancer or diabetes with a sermon? Hardly. Admonition, sincere though it may be, essentially denies that the patient is ill.

Sometimes pastors counsel when what the sick person needs more are psychiatric therapy and medicine that a minister cannot provide. There is a great difference between counseling and therapy. Counseling usually involves the giving of advice, whereas therapy helps a depressed person understand what she's experiencing mentally and emotionally, and helps her find a way to deal with it.

On the other hand, the pastor who is a quiet, steady, non-condemning presence provides great comfort. I recall how Reverend Henry DeMots, our minister at that time, comforted my wife when she told him, hesitantly, that she had quit praying because she felt God didn't listen anyway: "That's all right," he answered, "because we're all praying for you. That's what fellow believers are for." When an agonizing spiritual question came up, as it often did in my wife's battle, our minister served as lifeguard, throwing a rope to a drowning swimmer.

Seeking help early. I learned an important lesson through this experience: if you suspect that you or another family member has problems that need attention, don't wait too long to deal with them. Prompt attention makes a difference. In the last few decades, great advances have been made in the treating of depression, especially in the medicines prescribed. Today, especially with drug treatment, a depressed person can experience a measure of relief earlier in the sickness. And that enables him to begin therapy sooner.

It wasn't until my wife's five-year battle with depression that I learned — vividly and painfully — how sensitive, integrated, and complex a body and mind God gave to each of us. A thermometer can measure fever. An x-ray can show a broken bone. A biopsy can reveal a malignancy. But how does one measure the degree of fatigue or the depth of despair in a person suffering from depression? Today more and more is being learned about the complexity of the chemical systems in the human body and the imbalances that cause depression — and that means faster and better treatment. But it's still very important to seek help before the symptoms of depression are chronic and severe.

Family and friends. I learned early that everybody, absolutely everybody gets depressed at times. Almost everybody has a remedy too. But clinical depression as *illness* is not easily understood and even less easily accepted. Think of the typical responses people make when they hear that someone is depressed. *If she would only stop feeling sorry for herself. She should snap out of it. She should trust the Lord. She should count her blessings. She has everything; what more does she want?*

A most important first step for family and friends is to understand depression as an *illness* and to recognize the harsh effects it has on the depressed person and her family.

Depression scares people, especially when you start mentioning a psychiatrist or a mental hospital. Other illnesses evoke sympathy much more easily. Not that people don't care about the person who suffers from depression. They do — many care deeply. But because depression frightens them, and because they often know how to respond to a physical illness but not a mental illness, they don't know how to show their concern. A few observations may be helpful:

- Remember the family; depression is not an illness that occurs in isolation. Children often get shortchanged when one of their parents is ill. Offer to baby-sit for them, to take them to the movies or out for pizza. And remember that when one parent is hospitalized or is too ill to keep up with his or her "duties," it's difficult for the other parent to prepare good meals and maintain the house. Offer to fix dinner, vacuum the house, mow the lawn.

- Be frank in your queries. Depression is an illness. If you don't understand it, say so. Your sincerity counts most.
- Be sparing in sending get-well cards filled with pious phrases and books with instructions on positive thinking. A depressed person may not be able to handle them. A few sincere words of your own may help more.
- Call to ask if you can visit, and don't be offended if the answer is no.
- Allow the person to be ill, and understand that one of the symptoms of the illness is extreme mood fluctuations. Keep your visit short unless the person clearly indicates that she wishes you to stay longer.
- Dare to love. If you want to do something, follow your heart. Offer to visit with the spouse; bring a small treat to the depressed person; send notes *regularly*. The action may boomerang, but better that than not to have tried at all. Christ loved so much that he came to earth and to the cross; he didn't count the cost.
- Don't give up. It's hard to make a warm, positive impression on a depressed person — she's convinced she isn't worth your concern and attention. But a small thought or kindness expressed regularly may eventually get through — and it is therapeutic.

Living with a person who is depressed isn't easy. Trying to help a depressed person is very hard. Accepting depression as illness is an important first step. Understanding it, as the depressed person moves slowly forward — and sometimes backward — requires patience and faith in God's wisdom and compassion.

God *is* in control, and his love never fails.

APPENDIX C

How a Parent's Depression Can Affect Children

IN SPITE OF the extended and excellent therapy I received, my illness did affect the children. For one thing, I made a number of mistakes, even though I was determined not to. Sometimes, like my mother, I was too legalistic, too perfectionistic, too organized. I had so much to unlearn and relearn, and I practiced in and on my family. Besides environment (nurture), there was the genetic component (nature) that came into play. Indeed, two of my daughters were affected by a combination of these factors.

In 1979, long after I was initially treated for depression, a psychiatrist prescribed drugs for me that have stabilized me since then. At that time the psychiatrist suggested that I talk with my children about the probability that one or more of them may have inherited the disease, or at least a tendency toward it. He believed — and research has given increasing support to his theory — that depression is the result of a deficiency of particular brain substances called neurotransmitters, and that this deficiency can be inherited.

I followed his suggestion and did talk with my children then. But earlier I had already recognized, with much pain, that two of my daughters do struggle with depression. Although they have never required hospitalization and have always functioned well, they have both been helped by early recognition of the illness and doctor-supervised drugs.

Because genetically inherited chemical imbalances in the brain can usually be treated by prescribed drugs, it is probably the lesser of the two basic effects of a mother's depression on her children. But the influence of environment is less easily dealt with.

That has been true in my own situation. Medication alone has not taken care of all the psychological effects on my youngest daughter, Anita (who has given me permission to write about this).

Anita was born during my illness, which complicated things both before and after her birth. It is well known that the prenatal well-being of a child affects the child after he or she is born. Since I worried a great deal about the baby growing within me, praying anxiously that she would be born healthy, not stillborn, I'm sure this took its toll. Anita was also affected by how I treated her as an infant. For the several-month period after her birth until we returned to the States, I neglected her frequently. I failed to feed her when she was hungry. I failed to cuddle her when she cried. I failed to change her when she was wet. Only God knows whether I may have abused her even further during these months; I don't remember. I still think about this at times.

Anita, who is now a therapist and the program director for an adult chemical dependency program in a Colorado hospital, has said that yes, although she, as a preverbal infant, was unable to express her anger at being so neglected, the fact remains that she was a victim of genuine neglect. As an infant she had the need and the right to be fed, cuddled, and changed, and it is appropriate for her to be angry about having been

214

deprived of something she should have had. But at first Anita found it difficult to accept the validity of her feelings. When, in therapy, she identified her anger, she struggled with the guilt she felt for being angry at me because, as she said, her mother was sick and couldn't help it. But when she learned that anger at deprivation is legitimate no matter how that deprivation is caused, and she needn't feel *guilty* about her anger, she made progress.

Anita has also explained to me that another phenomenon of her early childhood affected her self-concept and self-esteem in much the same way that adoption affects children whose mothers give them up. The question, often buried in the subconscious, is, Why did my mother abandon me? Why didn't she want me? As a six-month-old baby, Anita was "abandoned" by her mother. When a man and a woman who were strangers to her came to her parents' door and offered to take care of her, her mother agreed. Her life then began all over again in a new environment where she learned to call these strangers "Papa" and "Mama." After two-and-a-half years in this situation, she was again "abandoned" — this time by Mama and Papa when they gave her back to Mommy and Daddy. Although Anita was considerably more verbal at this point, she was still unable to understand the complexity of these events. And Mommy was still going through her own struggles. (Although I was better, I was far from well.)

Experiencing such events as an infant and toddler makes a deep imprint on a child's psyche. When an individual develops psychological problems because of this kind of experience, there is a rational explanation for his or her thoroughly ambiguous self-identity and lack of self-esteem. But understanding and accepting this on an emotional level is more difficult, because the psyche is badly damaged and not easily persuaded. The effects of such experience not only linger but also impinge themselves on many other aspects of adulthood. The individual may struggle with such things as feeling lonely, forming relationships, and being self-confident.

When a parent is depressed, it is bound to affect the children in the family in certain ways. But prompt recognition and treatment of any problems can go a long way toward minimizing and correcting the damage.

Books That Have Helped Me in My Continuing Journey

Allen, Charles L. *God's Psychiatry: Healing of the Mind and Soul.* Westwood, N.J.: Fleming H. Revell, 1953.

This is a popular and helpful explanation of Psalm 23 that has been reprinted many times. But, although its basic premises are true, even rich, the book can mislead a reader into thinking that clinical depression is a "heal thyself" disease. It isn't.

Buechner, Frederick. *Telling Secrets.* San Francisco: HarperCollins, 1991.

This book is an expression of the author's need to tell of his father's suicide, his daughter's anorexia, and his own powerlessness to help. It gives a strong argument for Christians to share their burdens — because they "have much to do with the secret of what it is to be human."

Carlson, Kathie. *In Her Image: The Unhealed Daughter's Search for Her Mother.* Boston: Shambhala, 1990.

This book gives three very secular views of mothers and

daughters: the child's view (an egocentric viewpoint that evaluates the mother in terms of how her behavior affects the child); the feminist view (an adult viewpoint that sees the mother as an equal, a "sister," and allows for some empathic concern for her); and the transpersonal view (a revision of the child's view that allows for images other than the cultural stereotype of "mother" and no longer puts all "blame" on the mother). It provides some insights to help both mothers and daughters understand their relationship with each other. But its anti-Christian framework detracts from its usefulness for Christians.

Friday, Nancy. *My Mother, My Self: The Daughter's Search for Identity.* New York: Delacorte Press, 1977.

Besides the Bible and the three men God used in my life, this book has helped me most. It provided an insight about female sexuality that I sorely needed to help me understand my mother's training of her only daughter. I don't agree with many of Friday's premises, but I'm grateful for the light that her book shed on my problems.

Hesselink, I. John. *On Being Reformed — Distinctive Characteristics and Common Misunderstandings.* Ann Arbor, Mich.: Servant Publications, 1983.

The title of this book explains its content. It's an excellent corrective to the many myths that exist about John Calvin's interpretation of the Bible and Christianity.

Hoekema, Anthony A. *The Christian Looks at Himself.* Grand Rapids: William B. Eerdmans, 1975.

Dr. Hoekema examines what the Bible says about how we Christians should look at ourselves. Should we stress our continued sinfulness or our newness in Jesus Christ? Hoekema argues for the latter. We are God's "special creative act," he writes, "and [God] doesn't make junk." This is an excellent book — it helped me climb from the mental pit of "continued sinfulness" to "newness in Christ."

Hyder, O. Quentin. *The Christian's Handbook of Psychiatry.* Old Tappan, N.J.: Fleming H. Revell, 1973.

This is correctly called a "handbook." Dr. Hyder, a Christian psychiatrist, shares his professional insights about mental health, depression, and psychiatry in terms a layperson can understand. It can help "normal" Christians improve their own mental health, and it provides useful information for persons who live with individuals who are clinically depressed.

Lerner, Harriet Goldhar. *The Dance of Anger: A Woman's Guide to Changing the Patterns of Intimate Relationships.* New York: Harper & Row, 1985.

Anger need not deprive us of mental health. Goldhar offers a helpful (though secular) minicourse in understanding anger and using it as a positive force in living.

Low, Abraham A. *Mental Health through Will Training.* Boston: Christopher Publishing House, 1952.

This book, still being reprinted and widely used today, is the manual used by Recovery, Inc., an active, lay, mutual support system that has operated throughout the United States since the 1950s. No professionals are involved, and there is no fee. The book provides self-help techniques for people who are nervous, anxious, and depressed as well as people who are recovering from an emotional breakdown. While I was an outpatient and for three years after my hospitalization, I belonged to one of these groups. Although politics, sex, and religion are taboo subjects, the discussions and support of others who "really understood" helped me greatly. I have long dreamed of a similar voluntary group based on Christian principles.

Peck, M. Scott. *The Road Less Traveled: A New Psychology of Love, Traditional Values, and Spiritual Growth.* New York: Simon & Schuster, 1978.

This book offers a valuable approach to overcoming the suffering of mental illness. It would be helpful to anyone who has recovered enough to see his or her problems in perspective.

Smalley, Gary, and John Trent. *The Blessing.* New York: Pocket Books, 1986.

This is a book I wish both my mother and I could have read before we became parents. It's one all parents could benefit from. The authors articulate five elements of "blessing" that today's children need as much as did Old Testament children. Accordingly, the authors give parents the following suggestions: (1) make sure you engage in "meaningful touch" — hugging and so on — with your children; (2) tell your children how much you care about them (don't assume that they know you love them); (3) recognize how important your children are, and demonstrate to them how highly you value them; (4) picture a "special" future for your children; and (5) actively commit yourself to your children, assuming responsibility for "blessing" them (relying on God, of course, to give you strength and staying power).

Smedes, Lewis B. *Forgive and Forget: Healing the Hurts We Don't Deserve.* New York: Pocket Books, 1984.

Someone has said that "depression is anger turned inward." In many cases that's true. How do we forgive people who have hurt us and made us angry? This book offers a thoughtful and helpful exploration of forgiveness. Smedes says that "forgiving is love's toughest work and love's biggest risk." His wisdom can help readers forgive hurts and avoid turning anger inward.

Styron, William. *Darkness Visible: A Memoir of Madness.* New York: Random House, 1990.

This is an account by a gifted contemporary author of his "devastating descent into depression." His description is superb, although his struggle is without the component of spiritual warfare many Christians experience.

Timmerman, John H. *A Season of Suffering: One Family's Journey through Depression.* Portland: Multnomah Press, 1987.

This is a true and encouraging story of a family that stayed together while the mother was hospitalized for depression. This book will inspire any family members, but especially fathers, searching for help and support in a similar situation.

Van Leeuwen, Mary Stewart. *Gender and Grace: Love, Work and Parenting in a Changing World.* Downers Grove, Ill.: Inter-Varsity Press, 1990.

Although written many years after my experience, this book describes the fierce battle I fought concerning women and what I then called "kingdom work." What are women called to do in this world? Is their potential hindered by traditional roles and expectations? Van

Leeuwen enlightens the reader about the identity crisis that often underlies clinical depression in women.

Viscott, David S. *The Makings of a Psychiatrist.* New York: Arbor House, 1972.

This is Viscott's personal account of training to become a psychiatrist, but it reads like a novel. Viscott exposes some of the sham and callousness that is sometimes part of diagnoses, therapies, and yes, psychiatrists themselves. This is an interesting book that deepened my appreciation for dedicated Christian mental health workers on any level.

Vitz, Paul C. *Psychology as Religion: The Cult of Self Worship.* Grand Rapids: Wm. B. Eerdmans, 1977.

In this book Vitz offers a sharp criticism of secular counseling that often masquerades as a religion in which self is god. Of course, many non-Christians are excellent therapists, but Vitz helps any person who needs a psychologist or psychiatrist understand why committed Christian professional workers are a blessing.

Wetzel, Janice Wood. *Clinical Handbook of Depression.* New York: Gardner Press, 1984.

As the title indicates, this is an extensive handbook on clinical depression. It covers pathology, theories and models of clinical depression, suicide prevention, and more. Given its technical thoroughness, it is meant more for professionals than for lay readers.

Wiebe, Katie Funk. *Bless Me Too, My Father: Living by Choice, Not by Default.* Scottdale, Pa.: Herald Press, 1988.

Written for mature Christians, this book addresses change and spiritual development. It issues a warning as well as a challenge that we do not and cannot stand still. The past serves us for good or ill in the future. An excellent book.

Winter, Richard. *The Roots of Sorrow: Reflections on Depression and Hope.* Westchester, Ill.: Crossway Books, 1986.

This is an excellent and understanding book on both depression and hope. In no way is it a substitute for professional help, but it can, I think, help a Christian gain some insight into what the disease of depression is, and it does provide hope, which is sorely needed in the experience of depression.